Make Your Own Aphrodisiacs

Julie Bruton-Seal
& Matthew Seal

MERLIN UNWIN BOOKS

First published in Great Britain by Merlin Unwin Books, 2012

ISBN 978 1 906122 33 1

Published by:
Merlin Unwin Books Ltd
Palmers House
7 Corve Street, Ludlow
Shropshire SY8 1DB, UK

The authors assert their moral right to be identified as the authors of
this work

British Library Cataloguing-in-Publication Data:
A catalogue record for this book is available from the British Library

Designed and typeset in Palatino, Handwriting Dakota, Optima and Verdana
by Julie Bruton-Seal and Matthew Seal
Photographs by Julie Bruton-Seal
Printed by Leo Paper Products

Please note:
The information in *Make your Own Aphrodisiacs* is not intended to replace the
advice and care of a qualified medical practitioner. Heed the cautions given, and if
already taking prescribed medicines or if you are pregnant, seek
professional advice before using herbal aphrodisiacs

Contents

Know that these things favour coition: health, freedom from worry, absence of preoccupation, a cheerful disposition, a generous diet, wealth, and variety in the features and complexion of the woman.

– Sheikh Nefwazi, *The Perfumed Garden* (written 1420s)

Introduction

1. What are aphrodisiacs?

If you look the word up, aphrodisiacs are said to arouse or intensify sexual desire. This refers to Aphrodite, the Greek goddess of love in all its forms. There is a hint of 'love potions', something to make us fall in love. The goddess is patron of many plants and other products that help us in our search.

Anthurium: aphrodisiac by 'signature' but not in practice

The notion of aphrodisiacs includes our mental and emotional response as well as the physical pleasure of sexual intercourse. So the term is spacious enough to bring in desire, love and romance, mood and setting, libido and placebo.

Almost everything we eat has been considered aphrodisiac at some time in history. Anything new and exotic or expensive acquires a hint of the erotic – look at potatoes and tomatoes in Elizabethan Europe or maca today.

2. Do aphrodisiacs work?

If you go down the 'scientific' route, you will note a paucity of human clinical trials for even the most ancient of aphrodisiacs and conclude that there is little 'proof' that they work at all. If you go a more 'ethnobotanical' route, you'll take into account the continued use in traditional societies of many aphrodisiacs whether by shamans or society generally. If these plants don't work, why on earth would they continue to be used for thousands of years?

If it's all delusion and placebo, here's a thought: the word 'placebo' itself means 'I shall please'. Placebo is powerful, occurring both in scientific method and in issues of belief and conviction as part of efficacy. Write off placebo and you discard an entire mental/emotional aspect of how healing and loving alike are manifested.

This leads to the ancient idea of the doctrine of signatures. The way things

3. How do aphrodisiacs work?

The actions of the aphrodisiacs are subtle and multi-levelled. Many are **stimulants** – these may be hot plants, like chilli or pepper, which heat up the body and stimulate metabolisim, boosting circulation and bodily secretions. Other stimulants such as coffee and cola work on our nervous system.

The **fragrant aphrodisiacs**, like rose, jasmine and ylang ylang, also work via the nervous system. Smells have a powerful effect on our emotions, and a scent from long ago can take us back in an instant. Fragrances help arouse all our senses. Combined with touch in the form of massage with scented oils, they can be even more powerful.

Many of the aphrodisiacs we chose for this book are **rejuvenating tonics**, restoratives or *rasayana* herbs. Our sexuality is the peak of good health and vitality, so libido is often the first thing to go if we are tired or unwell. These vitality-restoring herbs are particularly helpful for anyone who is depleted, tired from working too hard or under long-term stress of any kind. Parents of young children may be young themselves but could really benefit from these herbs. We also tend to need them more as we get older.

Then there are herbs that work directly on our hormone levels to **increase**

Ginkgo is often included in aphrodisiac formulas for its circulation-enhancing properties. This particular tree also has breast-like growth on the branches, making it suggestive as well

looked was considered to give clues to how they could be used. In the case of aphrodisiacs, something that looks erotic can be arousing even if it lacks all aphrodisiac action. Hence the ancient and still persistent trade in rhino horn, tiger penises, bear paws, deer musk and so on that is driving so many animals to extinction. We do not accept these products as aphrodisiacs, and they have no place in this book.

libido, such as tribulus and shatavari. These are particularly useful during the andropause and menopause, when levels of sexual hormones drop in men and women respectively.

Last but not least are the **relaxing aphrodisiacs**, which go hand in hand with the restoratives. Often all we need is a little help to relax and unwind, letting go of the worries and preoccupations of the day. This may be a glass of red wine, some nutmeg, a shot of kava kava or making an aphrodisiac recipe.

Many of our chosen plants **improve sexual performance**, more obviously an issue for men. Many increase blood flow to the genitals, which helps with arousal in both sexes. The whole issue of erectile dysfunction (ED) needs addressing, if sales of Viagra and similar pills are anything to go by.

Medication such as that for high blood pressure can cause difficulties in this area, as can diabetes and other illnesses, and of course stress. The problem itself is the cause of much stress and embarrassment, so luckily many of our aphrodisiac herbs can help. Men are notoriously unwilling to discuss these issues, but the idea of making their own aphrodisiacs may tempt them.

Many of the herbs we discuss improve fertility in women and increase quality and volume of sperm in men.

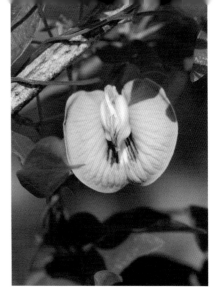

Clitoria: a wild, twining vine from southern India, but not an aphrodisiac, despite its name and appearance

4. Which are the best aphrodisiacs?

How did we compile our list? First, we looked at aphrodisiac traditions across the world, especially in India and China. Traditional Chinese Medicine texts go back some two thousand years, and aphrodisiacs like ginseng and horny goat weed were important then, as they remain today. Ayurvedic tradition in India is older still, with one of its eight disciplines being *Vajikarna*, the study of aphrodisiacs. Classic Ayurvedic herbs like ashwagandha, shatavari and ginger are used by herbalists East and West, and well deserve their inclusion here.

Chocolate, maca and chilli are from the New World, yohimbe and cola from Africa – each of them traditional aphrodisiacs and central to local culture, and now available everywhere.

Western traditions come in too, as in roses given to the beloved on Valentine's Day since at least Chaucer's time (died 1400). He wrote of the rose: *for this was sent on Saint Valentyne's day, when every foul cometh to choose his mate.*

Some plants are included here because we discovered their benefits ourselves years ago, like cnidium. Others are from perfumery, like jasmine, ylang ylang and the products of the orange tree. In all, we have evolved a list of our own favourite aphrodisiacs that are effective, are either food, medicine or perfume, are sustainable, have no or few side effects or toxicity (yohimbe is an exception), and which we can confidently recommend to you.

Asparagus spears: they look the part, and many eaters find they are

Many aphrodisiac books list animals, birds, fish and other non-plant aphrodisiacs. This book doesn't. We draw our personal ethical line at taking animal life for human pleasure.

We have attempted to describe in either our main or secondary lists all these most popular plant aphrodisiacs, and others that came lower down in our ranking. It's no more than a snapshot, but we hope a useful one.

5. Why make your own aphrodisiacs?

There are many good reasons. We know you can buy many of the herbs we list in pill or capsule form, and that they work, but taking a pill isn't very sexy. Wouldn't you rather make a wonderful dessert laced with ginseng that is beautiful and excites the taste buds? Or create a massage oil that transports you into another world, awakening sensuality and pleasure? Pills and capsules (and penis pumps) are just so clinical.

Another factor is that if you buy a quality dried herb from a herbalist or reputable supplier, you'll know what you're getting. You can smell it and taste it, and have the fun of thinking of creative ways to use it.

There is no quality control on aphrodisiac products sold on the Internet, and with a pill or a capsule it's hard to be sure. Expensive herbs are often substituted by cheaper ones, and sometimes pharmaceutical drugs are included in products claiming to be natural. Make your own aphrodisiacs from good ingredients, and you will be more than a passive, ill-informed buyer.

Making your own is also far cheaper, which is always helpful – we're sure you can think of something pleasurable to do with the money you save.

6. Is Viagra an aphrodisiac?

Viagra, Cialis, Levitra and their rivals are erection aids for men, not aphrodisiacs as such. This is not to say they don't have their uses and their followers. Since 1998, when Viagra was launched, upwards of a billion diamond blue pills have been bought and nearly 30 million men have used them. Within months Viagra became the most purchased drug ever.

These drugs are known as PDE-5 inhibitors, which work by relaxing the blood vessels in the penis, allowing blood to flood into it and cause a prolonged erection, even in men with seemingly permanent ED. The price is unpleasant side effects of upset stomach, headaches and flushing, with greater risks for men with either high or low blood pressure. There were a number of early fatalities with Viagra, now much reduced by tightening up the prescription conditions for doctors. There is little or no control on knock-off lookalikes sold online, or as yet on advertising claims there. Viagra is also the most counterfeited drug in history.

But, to be even-handed, Viagra has restored sexual life of some sort to men who had previously given up on it. Its very notoriety has helped people talk more freely about sexual problems, a revolution apparent in the shift in male terminology from 'impotence' to 'sexual dysfunction'. The equivalent female code-switch has been from 'frigidity' to 'loss of libido', and surely this is welcome progress.

7. Is alcohol an aphrodisiac?

A friend of ours says a glass of good red does it for her. Champagne drunk from a stripper's stilettos used to do it in Paris, we are led to believe. A glass or a pint sets up any beer drinker, but the reality is that hops in beer are oestrogenic and act as an anaphrodisiac for men. While a little beer is sexually stimulating and a man thinks he is irresistible, a lot proves he is not – 'brewer's droop' is an apt name. But men may not suffer performance anxiety at this point, being more likely to be asleep.

As we discuss for nutmeg and mace, the effect of alcohol is dose-dependent, so we say alcohol is aphrodisiacal up

to a point. That tipping point differs for each individual, and some people spend a lifetime enjoying finding it.

What we call 'Dutch courage' is nothing new. Chaucer again, on a bridegroom: *He drinkyth ipocras, claret and vernage,/ Of spyces hot, t'encreasen his courage.* Hippocras was a medieval favourite, a blend of warming spices and wine; even before then 'honeymoons' went better with the honey drink mead. Tinctures of herbs in alcohol remain part of the herbalist's armoury, and we include several in our recipes.

8. Are aphrodisiacs the same for men and women?

Technically some aphrodisiacs are 'women's herbs', like shatavari, and some are 'men's herbs', like ginseng and yohimbe. But many are adaptogens and most herbs are wise, so in practice we suggest you freely try any and every recipe we give and see what it does for you.

There needn't be a battle of the sexes over aphrodisiacs, but we do need to understand each other. Comedian Billy Crystal teases: *Women need a reason to have sex, men just need a place.* Comic writer Kathy Lette reveals: *For centuries men have wondered what a woman really wants in bed. I'll tell you: breakfast!* Let's be nice to each other. We are in this thing together, stress and all, age-ing and all. Any day is a possible Valentine's, any meal can be a love meal. If our loving is fulfilling, maybe we won't need aphrodisiacs anyway.

9. Are aphrodisiacs dangerous?

The writer Ovid was as much in favour of aphrodisiacs as the next wealthy Roman of two thousand years ago, but he did warn about *philtres which disturb the balance of the mind and illumine the fires of furious madness.*

Aphrodisiacs have always had a dark side, perhaps deriving from Aphrodite herself: one of her identities was Aphrodite Porne, the patron of prostitutes and love for sale, whose name is still recalled in 'pornography'.

The deadly link of aphrodisiac and poison, passion and toxicity has a long folk memory: the emperor Caligula's wife, and later Catherine de Medici and Lucrezia Borgia are only some of history's poisoners who beguiled their victims with fatal potions disguised

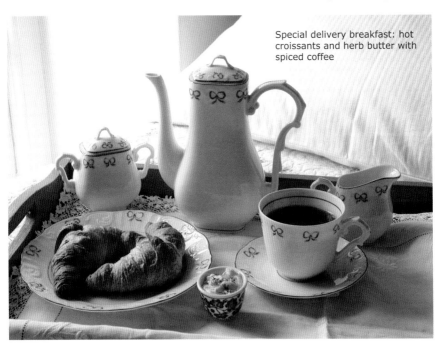

Special delivery breakfast: hot croissants and herb butter with spiced coffee

in alcohol or sumptuous aphrodisiac foods. The modern equivalent is the 'date-rape' drug Rohypnol.

We appreciate that the idea of danger is a turn-on in itself, and aphrodisiacs retain this *frisson*. We all know about the 'aphrodisiac of power' or 'aphrodisiac of money'. It's about influence and control as well as risk and danger.

We accept that, but we draw the line at poisons. Our notion of aphrodisiacs is far removed from the Marquis de Sade's in lacing chocolates with the deadly cantharides (the terrible Spanish fly) and watching several prostitutes suffer in agony – he was jailed for this stunt but not executed. Aphrodisiacs should not be something you put into somebody's food or drink without their knowledge and for selfish ends. Can't aphrodisiacs be shared in full awareness and informed consent in our own private time?

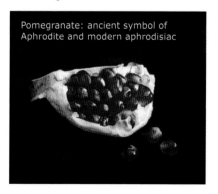

Pomegranate: ancient symbol of Aphrodite and modern aphrodisiac

10. Where do I get aphrodisiacs?

Sex shops don't sell aphrodisiacs as a rule, and doctors and pharmacists don't often prescribe them, so just where do you go? This book recommends you make your own, and as appealing foods or drinks rather than pills bought online. Some plants, like roses or jasmine, can be grown at home, but most need to be sourced as raw materials. For the more exotic plants check the suppliers listed in *resources*, page 93.

Your local herbalist will provide quality herbs as well as give you advice. Do be aware that in the UK a herbalist can only supply herbs after a face-to-face consultation – this can be brief, and is of course strictly confidential. Find a herbalist in the Yellow Pages, at your health store or complementary therapy clinic, or via the professional associations listed on our *resources* page.

Most purchasing of aphrodisiacs has been online, in an as yet unregulated marketplace. Along with sites offering Viagra and like products thousands tout 'herbal aphrodisiacs'. Some sites have good information but most don't, not even listing ingredients or risks. We advise you not to entrust such sites with your money and health.

Finally, don't rush it; give these plants time. In Mae West's words: *anything worth doing is worth doing slowly.*

Part 1
Make Your Own
APHRODISIACS

Ashwagandha

Ashwagandha is one of the most important tonics and aphrodisiacs in Ayurveda, the age-old medical system of India. It promotes sexual potency and sperm production

Ashwagandha, *Withania somnifera*, is a smallish shrub in the night-shade family whose root is the medicinal part. It is native to India and Africa

It is also called winter cherry and Indian ginseng

Generally very safe, although not recommend-ed in pregnancy and for people on sedatives or allergic to night-shade family species; minimal side effects, with no recorded drug interactions

- calming
- tonic
- adaptogen

Ashwagandha is a key herb in Ayurveda, India's 'science of life'. In Western terms ash-wagandha is an adaptogen (a class of plants that help a per-son adapt to stress and build overall immunity), as ginseng is. Indeed ashwagandha is sometimes called 'the Indian ginseng', although the two plants are not botanically related. It is as central to the Indian culture of health as ginseng is to China's.

Ashwagandha is equally diverse in its benefits, being used to treat exhaustion, loss of muscle tone, nervous disorders, depression and anxiety; it is high in usable iron, so is good for anaemia, and it is also a sedative (as *somnifera* in its Latin name suggests). In Ayurveda it is a *rasayana*, a rejuvenating plant that strengthens the life force and helps people recover zest for living. It is helpful to the old and to the young, and is a supporting presence for those recuperating from illness.

Above all in India ashwa-gandha is seen as a superb reproductive tonic for both sexes, and is the country's most powerful and popular aphrodisiac. While there is as yet little clinical evidence in the West to substantiate this use, as a sympathetic Ameri-can ethnobotanist notes, three thousand years and millions of satisfied patients is its own evidence. Why, he asks, study if people get wet when they take showers?

There can be little doubt that ashwagandha is an effective, safe and reliable aphrodisiac. It is far more than a sex aid – the beautiful thing about *rasayanas* and adaptogens is that they treat people rather than symptoms, invigorating the body, mind and psyche, bringing them into harmony.

As many stressed people know too well, loss of libido spirals down along with loss of self-esteem, fatigue and lack of interest in sex or anything much else. Ashwagandha is able to reverse the negative spiral and restore strength and a healthy libido, in a word sexual wellness, for both sexes, young or old. The central idea of vigour is captured in its Hindi name, which translates as 'strength of a horse' – a more generous and understanding version than the disparaging alternative sometimes seen in Western texts, 'smell of horse urine'.

The benefits of ashwagandha are most apparent if it is used regularly over a long period. It restores stressed adrenals and strengthens the whole body.

The powder is easy to incorporate in food. A herbalist friend has some in her porridge every morning, and it can be added to soups and smoothies. Do taste the powder before you add it to recipes, however, as it has a slight bitterness that does not go well with everything. We'd suggest starting with a smaller amount and building up as you get used to the flavour. Traditional preparations often include milk and ghee (clarified butter).

For massage, ashwagandha can be infused with sesame oil as a carrier. This creates a beautiful earthy oil, which because ashwagandha is an adaptogen can be deeply relaxing or stimulating, depending on circumstances.

Ashwagandha tincture

It is easy to make your own tinctures. Fill a jar with the herb (here **ashwagandha root**), then pour **vodka** in to cover it. Put the lid on and shake to remove bubbles, topping up if necessary. Keep in a cupboard for a month or so, shaking every few days. Strain and bottle. Take from 1 to 3 teaspoons daily.

Evening energizing cocoa

Ashwagandha root is traditionally boiled in milk as a drink. We like to combine it with cocoa to make an energizing and restorative evening drink. For each mug of **milk** or **almond milk**, use ½ to 1 teaspoon **ashwagandha powder**, 2 teaspoons **cocoa powder** (or to taste) and ¼ teaspoon **cardamom powder**. Bring just to the boil, then remove from heat. Add a little **vanilla extract** and sweeten with **honey** or **maple syrup**.

Cardamom

Cardamom is a tasty way to spice up your love life. It has a wonderful flavour that will complement both sweet and savoury dishes, and it has an ancient reputation as a warming and invigorating aphrodisiac

Elletaria carda-momum or Elachi is a tropical plant in the ginger family, native to south India. It is the seed pod and seeds that are used as a spice

Unusually, the pretty white flowers and green seed pods emerge from the plant's rhizomes

Safe for children and elderly, with no known inter-actions or toxicity

• mild stimulant

Cardamom is an ancient aromatic oil-yielding plant, which in its native south India is known as 'queen of spices' (pepper is 'king'). It was and is chewed as a favourite digestive and palate-cleanser, and as the go-to spice for all matters alimentary, from bad breath to diarrhoea. But an aphro-disiac?

It has long been regarded as such in Ayurvedic and Middle Eastern traditions. Modern research identifies one component of ripe car-damom seeds as 1.8 cineole. This compound is a central nervous system stimulant (in Indian terms, it gives 'diges-tive fire'), which also helps impart the attractive eucalyp-tus note to the aroma.

In Ayurveda cardamom is regarded as increasing sexual potency, and when added to coffee in the Middle East is either a drink to welcome guests or a mood-setter for lovers once guests have gone.

We have found that adding cardamom takes the 'jitteri-ness' out of coffee, and we grind up pods with the coffee beans, or make a masala chai with crushed cardamom seeds and other aromatics.

Cardamom is a warming and piquant addition to cakes, syrups and ice creams, and works well for savoury meals such as curries and rice. The best pods are lime green in colour, with black seeds and free from any tears in the outer husk.

Chai for lovers

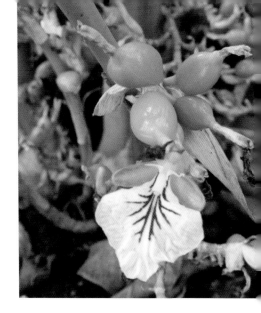

Grate a piece of **fresh ginger** 2 cm (about 1 inch) long into a saucepan. Add ½ litre (1 pint) **water**, 3 **cardamom pods**, crushed, 5 **black peppercorns**, a piece of **cinnamon stick**, and 2 or 3 **cloves**.
Heat and simmer for 10 minutes.
Add ½ cup **milk** and a rounded teaspoon of **tea**; simmer 10 minutes more. Strain. If you like, sprinkle a little **nutmeg** on top and add a few drops of **vanilla extract**. Sweeten with **honey**. Refreshing and satisfying, especially after lovemaking.

Cardamom syrup

This syrup is delicious on fruit salads, or simply poured over ripe mango. Crush 2 tablespoons of **cardamom pods**. Put in a saucepan with 2 cups **water** and simmer gently with the lid on for about half an hour.

Strain out the cardamom and return liquid to the pan. Add 1 cup **sugar** and bring to the boil, boiling until reduced by about half and the syrup begins to thicken. Add the juice of **half a lemon**, bring to the boil again, then remove from the heat and bottle.

Cardamom & cinnamon cocktail

Make **cardamom syrup** as above. Follow same process to make a **cinnamon syrup**, using a 10 cm (4 inch) **cinnamon stick**. Put equal amounts of the syrups in a glass, so that about ¼ of the glass is filled. Top up the glass with **soda water**, add **ice** and a pinch of **nutmeg** or **cola nut powder** (optional). As a variation, use a smaller glass and make it an alcoholic drink with a shot of your favourite.

Chilli

If you really want to heat up your love life, chillis are the obvious choice. They increase blood flow, and will help other aphrodisiacs get to where they're needed

Chilli is the hottest of hot herbs, with its very own heat-measuring scale (Scoville Units). Sweet peppers score 0 to 100 SU, cayenne and tabasco 30,000 to 50,000 SU; habanero at 100,000 to 300,000 SU is not even the hottest.

Clearly it pays to know your peppers: a chilli 'high' is one thing, but take the wrong-strength chilli for your constitution or state of health and you can incur unbearable pain from mouth to anus.

The active ingredient in chilli is capsaicin, whose effect is to open up cell membranes, triggering a pain mechanism that rapidly passes to other cells. But capsaicins are not just pain transmitters, they also open the blood vessels, easing the flow to peripheral organs, the hands or feet and genital areas. This is why chillis are good for rheumatism, lumbago or arthritis, including being rubbed on externally, why they help prevent clogging of arteries (atherosclerosis) and burn body fat, making them good in weight-loss diets.

Promoting better blood circulation is good news for aphrodisiac users, especially those with joint pain. Chilli also has benefits for heart health – reducing LDL, or 'bad' cholesterol, and equalizing blood pressure – more vitamin C than citrus and the capacity to kill pathogens in the body. It all means we should thank Christopher Columbus, who looked for India and pepper but found the Americas and chilli!

Stuffed chilli peppers

Slice large **chillis** in half lengthwise. (You can use long sweet peppers if chilli is too hot for you.) Remove the seeds. Sprinkle a few **pine nuts** into each, then fill with crumbled **cheese** and sprinkle with chopped **dill leaf**.
Bake in the oven at about 180°C (350°F) until the cheese has melted and is beginning to brown. Serve hot.

Fresh hot sauce

This sauce can be served to liven up any occasion and is delicious as an accompaniment to a variety of dishes. You can adjust the proportions to suit your taste buds. It will keep in the refrigerator for several days.

Take a few fresh red or green **chillis**, some cloves of **garlic** and a few chunks of fresh **ginger**. Put in a blender or food processor, adding enough **extra virgin olive oil** to blend into a paste.

Hint for hot chilli mouth: capsaicin is not water-soluble so water will not cool chilli heat, and indeed it might spread it; use alcohol, yoghurt or milk instead. Avoid the seeds, which have most capsaicin.

Chocolate

Theobroma cacao, the cocoa or cacao tree, is a small tropical tree native to Mexico and Central America

It is the seed (or bean) of the rugby ball-sized fruit that is used to make chocolate

Dark chocolate has been shown to be good for the heart

- euphoric
- stimulant

Chocolate: the world's favourite and universal aphrodisiac. Called 'the food of the gods', it is given on Valentine's Day as a symbol of love and as Easter eggs for fertility. But have you thought why it works so well?

Chocolate was originally taken as a bitter drink. In the pre-Colomban civilizations of South and Central America the beans were so valuable they were used as currency: money growing on trees.

Moctezuma, the Aztec king, was reported to drink 50 cups of a specially prepared foamy drink called Xocolatl every day from a golden goblet. This drink, made from cocoa beans with vanilla and chillis, reputedly gave him the strength and virility to keep the royal ladies happy.

Eating chocolate makes us feel happier, and not just because it tastes so good. One intriguing reason is that it melts at the same temperature as human body heat (34–38°C), giving it the special quality chocolatiers call 'mouthfeel'.

Chocolate has small amounts of the chemical phenylethyl-amine (PEA), which is a mild mood elevator. This is the chemical our brain produces in response to feelings of joy and love. Eating chocolate triggers these same feelings.

Chocolate's main alkaloid is theobromine, a heart stimulant. Chocolate also boosts serotonin levels. Serotonin is a neurotransmitter produced by the body, which acts as our brain's own antidepressant – another way that chocolate makes us feel good.

Dark chocolate and cocoa contain high levels of flavonoids, which act as powerful antioxidants in the body, mopping up free radicals and slowing our ageing. Recent research shows how flavonoids encourage vascular-wall health and the functioning of blood vessels, both significant for overall as well as sexual health.

Further, chocolate acts to lift endorphin levels in the brain. Endorphins are what flood the brain during times of peak physical exertion, creating the sensation of a permeating bliss, such as the 'runner's high'.

These positive health effects are most pronounced in chocolates that are high in cocoa and low in added sugar. We unashamedly recommend taking the elitist route, so forget mass market versions and go for quality. This is an affair of the heart!

The raw cocoa pod contains about 50 brown beans. The surrounding white pulp is sweet

Chocolate spice cake

Sift into a large bowl:
- 3 cups **plain unbleached flour**
- ½ cup **cocoa powder**
- 2 cups **sugar**
- 2 teaspoons **baking soda** (bicarbonate of soda)
- 1 teaspoon **salt**

Add:
- 2 cups **water** or **cold coffee**
- 2 tablespoons **vinegar**
- 2 teaspoons **vanilla extract**
- ½ teaspoon each **cinnamon** and **cardamom powder**
- ½ cup plus 2 tablespoons **vegetable oil** (olive, sunflower, etc)

Stir well and pour into 2 greased and floured 20 cm (8 inch) cake tins, or one larger heart-shaped tin and 8 or 10 cupcake cases.

Bake in a preheated oven at 190°C (350°F) for 30 minutes for the 20 cm tins. Cup cakes will cook in about 15 minutes, and larger tins may take up to an hour – test with a straw to see if they are done.

Cool on a cake rack, then remove from tins. Layer with **whipped cream** flavoured with **vanilla** and a pinch of **cinnamon**, or cover with ganache (recipe below).

Chocolate ganache

Ganache is simply chocolate and cream mixed together. The basic recipe uses roughly equal weights of chocolate and cream, but the proportions can be varied according to taste.

Bring 50 g (1¾ oz) **double cream** just to a boil and stir into 50 g (1¾ oz) of either grated or melted **dark chocolate**. Pour over cakes, dip fruit in it or let it set and use a melon baller to scoop out balls to roll in cocoa powder as truffles.

Cnidium

Cnidium seed is a Chinese aphrodisiac that can be eaten raw to great effect

Cnidium monnieri or She chuang zi is a Chinese member of the carrot family (Apiaceae)

Use the dried seeds

Also useful for skin problems

- stimulant
- increases libido
- improves performance

Cnidium looks like a typical member of the carrot family, with the usual white umbrella of small blossoms. The seeds are small, flat and light brown.

Nothing spectacular so far, but please taste the seeds: a pinch begins as bland, if nutty, and turns into something like celery seed and then dill. All the time the taste grows warmer, more tingling and numbing, leaving the mouth and whole digestive system awakened. The effect goes deeper still to the sexual organs, working quite quickly, and it lasts for hours.

This is a traditional Chinese aphrodisiac, *She chuang zi* or snake bed plant, that is not much known in the West. More Internet aphrodisiac formulas now use it (often with dodder and schisandra), and we rate it highly.

Others share this view: in a random test of several aphrodisiacs on half a dozen friends, all put cnidium over yohimbe, a much more reputed herbal aphrodisiac. Both males and females reported a definite rapid increase in libido and energy.

Cnidium is also used externally (the seeds are ground up in water) in China as an intimate wash; it is effective too in this form for treating eczema and ringworm.

We find taking cnidium is simplicity itself: just chew or swallow a teaspoonful of the seeds, which you can buy from your herbalist or in an Oriental health store. Try grinding the seeds and sprinkle on food as a condiment, for soups, stews or in a salad dressing. But, as the raw seed is so good, why bother with other versions?

Cola, kola, goora
or guru nut,
*Cola nitida, C.
acuminata*, Ster-
culiaceae family

A large tropical
tree native to
West Africa, now
also grown in
tropical South
America; creamy
white flowers
with red centres
are followed by
pods containing
fleshy white or
red seeds, the
'nuts'

Use the powder
or tincture

Also medicinal
for diarrhoea
and dysentery,
asthma and
bronchitis

• stimulant

Avoid in
pregnancy and
in cases of
hypertension,
but it is generally
safe in moderate
quantities. No
reports of toxicity
or drug inter-
action problems

Cola nut

*Cola nut will be most familiar for its use in
soft drinks bearing its name, but has valuable
stimulant, tonic and aphrodisiac effects. It
has the ability to stimulate and strengthen at
the same time*

Cola (or kola) is known as
a 'nut' but is the seed of a
large West African forest tree.
The nut has been chewed as
a stimulant, digestive and
aphrodisiac in western and
central Africa for thousands
of years, and its use was
central to traditional life-
cycle celebrations. In Hausa
society, for example, a bride's
mouth was touched with cola
on her wedding night.

Cola nut, used either dried
or fresh, contains three
stimulants: theobromine (as
in chocolate), caffeine (as in
coffee) and kolanin. Its level
of caffeine is higher than that
of coffee (about 3% as against
2%), and cola is sweetly
astringent, which made it an
excellent ingredient for the
newly developed Coca-Cola

Cola flowers

in 1886 and Pepsi-Cola in
1893. Most of the cola crop
still goes into soft drinks
worldwide, where it adds
colour and 'pep' as well as an
earthy flavour.

Medicinally, cola acts as a
moderate central nervous
system and heart stimulant,

with an uplifting quality that makes it a wonderful antidepressant. Its stimulant effect is balanced by its earthy, grounding and strengthening nature.

It has a traditional use in staving off fatigue, hunger and thirst (much like coca in South America), with a feel-good settling of the stomach and stressed or worried minds. As such it promotes the appetite in all senses and enhances bodily energy and awareness.

Cola has a low-key reputation as an aphrodisiac but we rate it highly for taste, uplift and invigoration.

Cola coffee

Cola combines really well with coffee, adding an earthy depth. Add a teaspoon of **cola powder** to enough **coffee** for two people. Brew as normal. A little cinnamon, a few pods of cardamom or a piece of vanilla bean can also be ground with the beans for added flavour and aphrodisiac effect.

Cola decoction

Put in a saucepan: 2 cups **water** and 1 tablespoon **cola powder**
Bring to a boil, turn down heat, cover and simmer gently for 10 minutes.
Strain through a cloth when cool.
Add 2 tablespoons per cup of **apple juice** or **sparkling apple** or **white grape juice.**

Real cola

4 cups **water**
2 tablespoons **cola powder**

Bring to a boil, turn down
heat, cover and simmer gently
for 10 minutes.
Strain through a cloth.
Pour back into a clean
saucepan, add 1 cup **sugar**.
Boil for about 5 minutes.
Cool.
Add the juice of half a **lemon**
¼ teaspoon **vanilla extract**
Add **sparkling water** to taste.

Damiana

Damiana is a superb tonic for both sexes. It is a pleasant-tasting herb that can be simply taken as a tea, or incorporated into more exotic recipes, though some people prefer to call it a 'nervine' rather than an aphrodisiac

The herbal literature is undecided whether damiana is an aphrodisiac, with few human clinical trials yet addressing the issue. This academic doubt is recent, as previous generations, and medical officialdom, were happy to name this plant after the sixteenth-century herbal pioneer, William Turner, and acknowledge its main use, as *Turnera aphrodisiaca*. The famous British herbalist, Mrs Grieve, writing in 1931, still used this name, but modern taxonomy specifies *Turnera diffusa* var. *aphrodisiaca*.

Incidentally, the common name damiana has even more distinguished origins, being a tribute to Damian (martyred in AD 303), the patron saint of pharmacists.

The ancient Maya peoples of Central America used damiana as an aphrodisiac. Most Mexicans today have no problem in regarding damiana as a direct sexual stimulant and antidepressant for both sexes. It is also the main ingredient of a popular alcoholic cordial, sold in bottles the shape of women's torsos, in Mexico and the US.

Damiana has a pleasant taste, aromatic and slightly sweet, that is refreshing as a simple tea or can be adapted well to more exotic recipes. We find it mixes well with liquorice and rose, a combination that enhances its restorative and hormone-balancing properties. It is also a good addition to chillis and garlic in savoury dishes.

Damiana, *Turnera diffusa*, is a Central American plant with pretty yellow flowers. It is harvested while flowering, so the dried herb will be leaves, stems and flowers

Also used for depression, anxiety, spasms, urinary complaints, diabetes and menstrual problems

Warming and drying

- tonic
- increases libido
- calming
- hormone balancing

Avoid during pregnancy. May reduce blood sugar levels, so exercise caution if you have hypoglycaemia

Damiana & liquorice tea

Mix roughly equal parts: dried damiana and dried liquorice root. If you like a sweeter tea, use more liquorice.
Use a heaped teaspoonful per cup of boiling water, cover and steep for about 5 minutes. Strain and drink.

Damiana iced tea

Mix 2 heaped teaspoons damiana, 1 heaped teaspoon mint, and some rose petals. Pour boiling water on them, brew for 5 minutes. Strain and chill. Serve over ice.

You will feel the most benefit from damiana with regular use as a daily nerve and hormonal tonic, which builds its full effect over several weeks.

Mexicans, old and new, believe that damiana is an effective and safe aphrodisiac that has no reports of toxicity.

Damiana butter sauce

Melt 50 g (1¾ oz) **butter**. Add 1 heaped teaspoon **dried damiana** and infuse for about 10 minutes. Dried damiana is often a bit woody, so strain the melted butter into a clean dish, then add 1 **clove crushed garlic** and about 1 teaspoon **crushed green chili**, or to taste.
Dip artichoke leaves or freshly steamed asparagus in it, or serve over your favourite aphrodisiac dish.

Rose & damiana elixir

Fill a jar half full with fragrant **rose petals**, add 3 tablespoons **dried damiana**, a tablespoon each of **ashwagandha** and **shatavari root** (optional), and a stick of **cinnamon**. Fill to half or ¾ full with **brandy** (or vodka) and fill the rest of the way with **honey**. Leave for 4 to 6 weeks, shaking or stirring occasionally, then strain and bottle. Have a liqueur glassful as desired.

Figs

Figs are succulently suggestive of sex and fecundity

Figs may have been the real 'apple' in the Garden of Eden, while fig leaves were the modest coverings for Adam and Eve after they ate the forbidden fruit. Some see ripe figs as male in shape and, when cut, exposing the multiple seeds encased in pulpy flesh, as female and fertile; others say the opposite. The favourite fruit of Cleopatra, it has been used as an aphrodisiac wherever it is grown – forbidden or not!

D.H. Lawrence's 1923 poem 'Figs', excerpted here, comes closer than most to the heart of its (and his) sexuality:

Fig, fruit of the female mystery,
covert and inward,
Mediterranean fruit, with your
covert nakedness,
Where everything happens
invisible, flowering and fertilisation, and fruiting
In the inwardness of your you,
that eye will never see
Till it's finished, and you're
over-ripe, and you burst to give
up your ghost.

Although wonderful cooked in roast dishes as a glaze, figs are irresistible fresh and ripe. Pick from the tree on a hot day (steal the figs from the wasps if necessary) or gently heat seasonally-bought figs in the oven. The rich, creamy filling of our recipe contrasts the sweetness of orange juice and liquorice with the spicy tang of black pepper.

While dried figs can be soaked and warmed, they don't look or taste as good as the real thing. Make the most of figs' ripeness in season!

Stuffed figs

Mix in a small bowl:

        50 g (1 ¾ oz) **cream cheese**
        ½ tablespoon **orange blossom water**
        ½ tablespoon **epimedium tincture**
        ½ teaspoon **liquorice root powder**
        ¼ teaspoon freshly ground **black pepper**

Select 2 ripe fresh figs. Make two slices in each fig from the top, almost to the bottom, to create an X. Spoon or pipe the mixture into the centre of each fig, squeezing the sides together gently to hold it firmly. Chill them until you are ready to eat them.

Ginger

Ginger is equally a spice, a food, a drink and a medicine. Its characteristic is heat: warming to hot in the fresh rhizomes and hot to very hot when dried into powder

Ginger root,
Jamaica ginger,
*Zingiber
officinale*

Tropical, grown
from South
America (Brazil
is the major
producer) to
India, China and
SE Asia.
Underground
rhizomes are
used medicinally;
flowers can be
eaten

Use fresh ginger
or the dried
powder

One Ayurvedic
writer describes
ginger as 'the
herbalist's best
friend'; an anti-
inflammatory and
anti-bacterial,
used for 'flu,
fevers and
colds, nausea,
diarrhoea, raising
'digestive fire',
and inducing
sweating

• stimulant

Ayurveda in India and Traditional Chinese Medicine recognize different uses for fresh and dried ginger and give them different names. In Western terms, fresh ginger gently increases peripheral blood circulation, including to the genital areas, and lowers blood pressure; dry ginger is stimulating from the heart outwards, and is more used to treat cardiac conditions and for its blood-thinning properties.

On this basis fresh ginger is more directly aphrodisiac but both forms are used wherever ginger grows or is marketed. It can be grated over savoury or sweet food and taken as a tea (with honey) indefinitely and safely, with pleasure and without side effects.

Research has shown that atherosclerosis (clogging) of the penile artery is the cause of half the cases of erectile dysfunction in men over 50. Ginger, garlic and chillis are among the foods that can reverse or reduce this depressing statistic, and deserve to be thought of as daily aphrodisiac aids.

Ginger grenadine

Pour the juice of a **lemon** and a cup of **apple juice** into two tall glasses; top up with real **ginger ale**. Add **ice**. Slowly pour in **grenadine** to create shades of light and dark in the glass.

Hot ginger sauce

Grate 1 piece **ginger**, about 1½ inches (3 cm) long, and crush 2 cloves **garlic** and about a teaspoon fresh **chilli**. Add a teaspoon of **galangal** powder if you have it. Fry these together gently for a few minutes in **coconut oil** or **toasted sesame seed oil**. Add a small cup of **coconut milk**, some chopped **basil** or **coriander leaves**, a little **soy sauce**, and the juice of a **lime** or half a **lemon**.

This is a delicious sauce for stir fries, steamed vegetables or curries.

Green masala

Grind up a small piece of fresh **ginger**, 1 or 2 cloves of **garlic**, 3 or 4 fresh **green chillis** and a small bunch of **fresh coriander leaves (cilantro)** with a little **water** to make a paste.

Serve this masala as a condiment or in cooking – use your imagination.

Ginseng

Ginseng has an ancient reputation as an aphrodisiac and rejuvenating tonic. It invigorates and energizes mind and body, and improves sexual performance. The best ginseng roots, sometimes decades old, fetch very high prices

The Chinese name for ginseng, *ren shen*, means 'man root'. Ginseng is a plant that conjures up the mysteries of the Orient, but surprisingly vast quantities of ginseng have been exported from North America to China from the early nineteenth century. The American form is similar to the Asian species, both as a plant and in its effects.

Ginseng invigorates the mind and the whole body, reducing fatigue and building vitality and endurance. It improves erectile function and increases male fertility, especially among the elderly. Normalizing immune function, it is used to treat a wide range of conditions. It is particularly useful for depletion caused

by overwork, stress or illness, and can be used by both sexes if energy levels are low.

Asian ginseng is one of the most studied herbs in the world, so there is plenty of modern evidence from human research to support the traditional claims.

Roots are usually harvested when the plant is 5 to 12 years old, which is one reason they are so expensive. As with any high-price herb, substitutions are often made, and commercial ginseng drinks probably contain too little root to be therapeutic.

Ginseng root is white when harvested. The red Asian root has undergone a process of

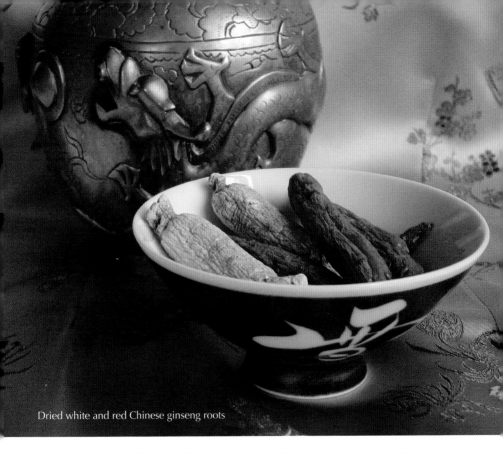

Dried white and red Chinese ginseng roots

curing that gives it the red colour and makes it more heating and stimulating. Herbalists generally consider the American ginseng less heating than the Asian, and more suited to women and younger people.

It is thought that ginseng increases nitric oxide levels in the penis, as does Viagra, thus promoting blood flow and subsequent erection. Ginseng is safer (and usually cheaper) than the drug and is more natural.

The easiest way to take ginseng is simply to chew on a few bits of the cut root. Initially the taste is a little bitter, but as you chew and the root dissolves in your mouth it leaves a lingering and energizing sweetness.

You can make a really good-quality ginseng extract by using the tailings, or small side roots, which are much cheaper to buy than the large roots. Below are three different types of fresh ginseng roots (from the left): Asian, Japanese and American.

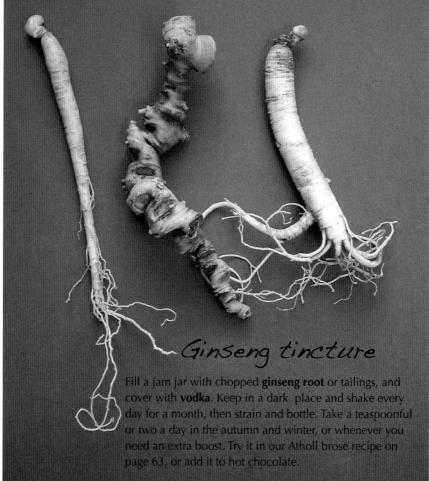

Ginseng tincture

Fill a jam jar with chopped **ginseng root** or tailings, and cover with **vodka**. Keep in a dark place and shake every day for a month, then strain and bottle. Take a teaspoonful or two a day in the autumn and winter, or whenever you need an extra boost. Try it in our Atholl brose recipe on page 63, or add it to hot chocolate.

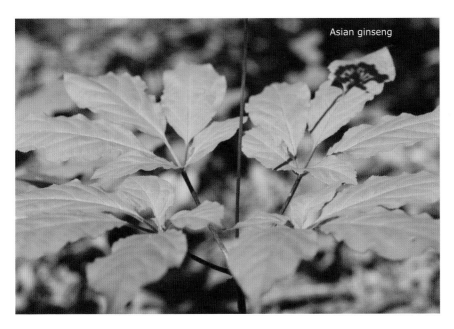
Asian ginseng

Ginseng & schisandra tea

Mix roughly equal parts **ginseng root, schisandra berry** and **liquorice root**. Use a tablespoon of the mix to two cups **water**, cover and simmer gently for 10 minutes.

Strain and drink either hot or chilled.

Ginseng electuary

Mix 2 tablespoons **ginseng powder**, 1 tablespoon **liquorice powde**r and 1 teaspoon **cardamom powder** with enough runny **honey** to make a soft paste (electuary). This keeps quite well in a jar. Take a spoonful daily or for an occasional energy boost.

Horny goat weed

This ancient and reputable Chinese aphrodisiac has become hugely popular in Western health stores and on the Internet. Is this all hype, or does horny goat weed work as well as its name promises?

Horny goat weed was by far the most frequent ingredient in our straw poll of 100 Internet sites selling herbal aphrodisiacs and which listed constituents (see page 87). It had hits in just over half of the sites sampled, with the next one, ginseng, registering a third.

Does this make horny goat weed the best current aphrodisiac – or is this hype, wishful thinking, placebo? The name is a marketing dream, but this translation of *yin yang huo* is not the only one: the leading book in English on Chinese herbal medicine renders it 'licentious goat wort'. Would that have hit the jackpot too?

The name is from the tale of a Chinese goatherd who found his goats, or in some versions a monster called yin yang, became sexually insatiable when eating the leaves of a low-growing plant. Incidentally, you may have horny goat weed growing in your garden as Epimedium, an attractive perennial ground cover.

This is a reputable kidney and liver tonic, and it needs time to work through and tonify your whole system. Take daily as a tea, liqueur or tonic formula for, say, four to six weeks and don't expect immediate results. It is proven to increase sperm count and harden erections, and is a libido enhancer in women, so is worth waiting for.

Horny goat weed tea

Put 2 tablespoons of dried **horny goat weed leaves** in a teapot and pour in 2 mugfuls of **freshly boiled water**. Cover and let steep for about 5 minutes, then strain, pour into two mugs and drink together. It has a slightly sweet taste that is warming and pleasant. Can be used cold in a cake icing.

Horny goat weed liqueur

Loosely fill a large jar with dried **horny goat weed leaves**.
Add: a slice or two of **orange**
       3 or 4 **cardamom pods**
       1 tablespoon **brown sugar**
Pour in enough **whisky** to fill the jar and submerge the contents. Put the jar in a warm dark place for two weeks then strain and bottle.
Enjoy a small liqueur glassful, sipped slowly.

Tonic aphrodisiac formula

This is a formula made from herbal tinctures, but can easily be adapted to using powdered dry herbs in the same proportions.

Mix 6 parts **epimedium**, 5 parts **damiana**, 5 parts **ashwagandha**, 4 parts **muira puama**, 3 parts **saw palmetto** and 2 parts **liquorice** tinctures. (Each part can be taken as 10 ml, a teaspoon or any measurement of your choice.)

Dose: 1 teaspoonful three times a day.

Jasmine

The fragrance of jasmine is euphoric, heady and sensuous – smelling the flowers or dabbing the oil (absolute) on the tip of your nose is blissful. Jasmine has always been associated with love and weddings. It is prized by perfumiers for the way it combines muskily masculine and florally feminine qualities, the sensuous and spiritual

Jasmine's aphrodisiac qualities are related to its fragrance, and any of the fragrant species can be used. *Jasminum officinale* is the hardiest, while *J. grandiflorum* is most often used for perfume and *J. sambac* is generally used to flavour teas

In Hindu folklore, the god of love annointed his arrow tips with jasmine oil before piercing the hearts of lovers. Jasmine was used by lovers in ancient Persia to perfume their bodies, and jasmine is a symbol of divine love and longing for spiritual union in Sufi poetry.

Jasmine is unique in the way it encompasses apparent opposites. It is both muskily masculine and florally feminine. It is earthy and enlightening, sensuous and spiritual, yin and yang. It has been associated with the moon and with Jupiter, and has been called both 'king of perfumes' and 'queen of perfumes'. It is considered by some to be warming and by others to be cooling, and is used in fragrances for both men and women.

Emerging into full glory after sunset, jasmine is the fragrance of warm, steamy nights. It is euphoric, rich, heady and sensuous. The scent of jasmine instantly makes you feel happier. If have a garden, plant jasmine and strew fresh jasmine flowers over your pillows, where they will release their perfume all night long.

We were in central Cyprus a few years ago, renting a house in an orange orchard. All day long the scent of orange flowers permeated the air. At night, though, a single jasmine plant overwhelmed every other scent. It was exactly as Keats wrote in *Endymion*, a lover's poem if ever there was:

It was a jasmine bower, all bestrown
With golden moss. His every sense had grown
Ethereal for pleasure.

Jasmine flowers are edible, and will flavour sensuous dishes to tempt the palate. Their slight edge of bitterness balances the sweetness of their scent.

Jasmine is heat-sensitive, and the essential oil cannot be extracted with steam as it is for most flowers. The perfume was traditionally made by enfleurage, a lengthy process that layers the flowers on top of a cold purified fat, then extracts the scent in alcohol. It is very labour-intensive, hence costly.

Today, most jasmine oil (absolute) is extracted chemically with solvents. It is still very expensive: 8,000 jasmine flowers yield only one gramme of absolute. Use jasmine absolute as a perfume, alone or mixed with other heady scents, and as a sensuous addition to massage oils.

Jasmine oil

You can make your own natural jasmine oil easily at home if you have a flowering vine.

Melt a thin layer of **coconut oil** on a non-stick baking tray. Allow it to solidify at room temperature, then lay a layer of **fresh jasmine flowers** over it. This works best if the flowers are picked in the evening or early in the morning, when their scent is strongest. Cover the flowers with a sheet of wax paper.

Replace the flowers with fresh ones every couple of days. After a week or two, the oil should have a good scent of jasmine. It is not nearly as strong as an absolute, but is made without solvents.

It can be used as a perfume and is a wonderful oil for the face or to massage the body.

Jasmine fruit salad

Put in a bowl together:
        ½ cup **cherries**, halved and pitted
        ½ cup **Cape gooseberries**, halved
        ½ cup **green seedless grapes**
        1 tablespoon **jasmine flowers**
Mix well. Drizzle with **honey** or **cardamom syrup**
(page 19) and serve.

Crystallized jasmine flowers

Put in a small jar:
>   **2 tablespoons** rosewater
>   **1½ tablespoons** gum arabic

Put the lid on and shake well. Leave overnight for the gum to fully dissolve.
Pick jasmine flowers, ideally in the early morning when their scent is strongest.
Use a fork to dip the flowers into the rosewater solution, then shake off the excess.
(If you are doing a large batch, it works well to put the flowers on a saucer to
drain while you dip more flowers.)
Lay each flower on caster sugar **in a small bowl, and sprinkle sugar over the flower**
so that it is thinly coated, then place the flower on a baking tray to dry. When
you've finished dipping all the blossoms, place the tray in an airing cupboard to
dry for a few days. Once crisp, the flowers can be stored in an airtight container
until you are ready to use them.

Jasmine tincture with ice cream

Choose a good vanilla-flavoured ice cream **or ice cream subsitute.**
Scoop into two small bowls. Pour a teaspoon or two of jasmine
tincture **over, and decorate with** crystallized jasmine flowers.

Jasmine pudding

Put in a small saucepan: 1 tablespoon **jasmine tea**
Pour on 75 ml (2½ fl oz) **boiling water**, and leave to infuse for 1 minute.
Add 30 g (1 oz) **caster sugar**
150 ml (¼ pint) **single cream**
Slowly bring to a boil, stirring over low heat. Check the taste until the cream is well flavoured. Strain the cream into a clean saucepan.
Dissolve 1 teaspoonful **agar** in ½ tablespoon **water**, and add to the cream. Simmer gently until the agar has dissolved. Pour into two dessert dishes and chill until set. Decorate with fresh jasmine flowers, if available.

Maca

Maca is an unlikely candidate as an aphrodisiac: an unspectacular root crop grown high in the Andes, it resembles a turnip or swollen radish, but has become an Internet sensation

Maca or Peruvian ginseng is the tuber of the plant *Lepidium meyenii*, an Andean crop in the cabbage family

Use powder or tincture

- tonic
- performance enhancing
- stimulant

Thriving high up where no other crops survive in poor soils and freezing, windswept weather, maca is a traditional source of nourishment for man and beast alike in the Peruvian mountains, where, to their surprise, the Spanish *conquistadors* found 'well-fed babies and tall adults'.

Local people attributed their health and fecundity to a diet of baked or boiled maca, which also helped the Spanish horses regain strength and fertility. Inca warriors were given maca to increase their martial ardour; after conquering a town, they were forbidden more maca, to protect the local women from their amorous attention.

Maca is often promoted as 'Peruvian ginseng', though the two species have no botanical relationship. They do reportedly share such medicinal benefits as metabolic and mental stimulation, steroidal hormone balancing, recovery from fatigue, and libido enhancement for both sexes (notably for men with erectile dysfunction and women at menopause). So great is the Internet interest in maca and its enthusiastic hyping that its sustainability as a Peruvian export crop is under threat.

Maca is thought to be so aphrodisiac because of high amino acid levels. Research highlights two: maca's arginine helps produce nitric oxide, which increases sperm production and activity, and its histidine assists successful ejaculation. Maca does not add testosterone, contrary to the claims of some websites.

Maca is a staple food, remember, and its benefits are cumulative over long periods; it is not an instant drug. The powder smells like butterscotch, but blander and slightly bitter. Drinking maca powder stirred into fruit juice or water makes the scalp tingle. Add it to porridge, breads and cakes, and see why the Andeans enjoy it.

Maca cupcakes

Warm together: ½ tablespoon **vinegar**
                    1 tablespoon **golden syrup**
                    4 tablespoons **butter**
                    ½ cup **light brown sugar**
When soft, beat until creamy.
Add: ½ cup **milk** or **oat milk**
           1 cup **plain white flour**
           2 tablespoons **maca powder**
Mix until well blended.
Pour: 1 tablespoon **boiling water**
over   ½ teaspoon **bicarbonate of soda** (baking soda)
and stir into the cake batter.
Pour into 10 muffin cases and bake at 180°C (350°F) for 15 to 20 minutes, until golden on top and cooked through. Cool.
Alternative: also delicious with 2 teaspoons ginger powder instead of the maca.

with vanilla fudge icing

Melt 1 teaspoon **butter** in a saucepan.
Add: 1½ cups **sugar**
           ½ cup **milk**
           ½ teaspoon **salt**
Stir until it reaches boiling point. Continue cooking until the mixture reaches the soft ball stage (115C°, 240°F). Cool a little, add ½ teaspoon **vanilla extract** and beat until smooth, then spread on the cup cakes. If the icing gets too stiff, warm it over hot water. Decorate the top of each cupcake with a small, very ripe **strawberry** while the icing is still soft.

Matthew says he loves the combination of hard, sweet icing, a soft, light cake and luscious strawberry melting in the mouth, and we think you will too.

Mango

A ripe mango, especially warm from the sun, is a sensuous succulent pleasure to eat. The rich flavours and smooth texture caress the mouth. How could such pleasure not be aphrodisiac?

Mangos are the fruit of a tall, long-lived tropical tree, *Mangifera indica*. There are many different varieties, each with their own unique characteristics (Alphonso is top-rated in India) but we've yet to taste one that wasn't delectable

• sweet & succulent

There is an episode of *Seinfeld* where Kramer gives George a piece of mango to try. George, forever sceptical, first just says it's juicy and ripe, then after a few seconds shouts out: 'It's like a shot of B_{12} – it's a taste explosion!' He goes for the biggest piece.

Our advice would be to follow George. Mango flesh in season has the colour of sunshine and the ambrosia of honey. It is messy, deliciously so, and you are bound to get juice on your chin and strings in your teeth. You will probably gnaw the stone to extract every last taste. It doesn't matter, have another.

When it's summer and mango fever strikes, as we hope it will, the only practical thing to do – and this is our main mango recipe – is to eat it while naked, preferably in a hot bath, sharing at least the water with your loved one.

Mangos are good green too, when the flesh is sourer and more acid. *Amchar* is mango powder that gives a tang to samosas, chutneys and curries. The green fruit is drying, antibacterial and rich in vitamin C, whereas the mature fruit has more vitamin A (sorry, George, not B_{12}). Sweet mango goes into jams and a mild chutney, but as a fruit it is incomparable.

The taste of ripe yellow mango is hard to describe, but that doesn't deter all authors.

Mango with cardamom syrup

E.J. Banfield made a worthy attempt in his 1911 memoir, *My Tropic Isle*. It's the book's centenary as we write:

Take of a pear all that is mellow, of a peach all that is luscious, of a strawberry all that is fragrant, of a plum all that is kindly, of an apricot all its aroma, of cream all its smoothness. Commingle with musk and honey, coriander and aniseed, smother with the scent of musk roses, blend with cider, and the mixture may convey a dim sense of some of the delectable qualities of one kind of mango.

How to ripen your mango
Put it in a brown paper bag, by itself or with an apple or banana. It's ready when it has a sweet aroma and the flesh gives a little on gentle pressing.

Slice down either side of the flat stone, (the stone is at the widest part of the fruit), cut in cubes down to the skin, then turn the skin out to expose the flesh. Delicious just as is, or pour cardamom syrup (page 19) or passion fruit pulp over the mango before devouring.

Muira puama

This Amazonian tree is known as potency wood, its bark and roots having a long-standing reputation as an aphrodisiac

Muira puama is called 'potency wood', referring to the local use of its powdered bark and roots as an aphrodisiac drink and tincture for both sexes. It is recognized as an aphrodisiac in Brazilian herbalism, and has been used in a low-key way in Europe since at least the 1930s, though its reputation is currently gathering pace. Another Amazonian species, *Liriosma ovata*, is also called 'muira puama' but has different medicinal effects.

Muira puama appears to be a safe, powerful aphrodisiac without reported side effects (apart from overstimulation leading to sleeplessness in some cases), toxicity or drug/plant interactions – though as yet there have been few human clinical trials.

The plant's active constituents are not water-soluble in heat, which means that even a long decoction will not extract them as effectively as an alcoholic tincture.

One European writer has suggested this recipe for a muira puama cocktail – combine 5 tablespoonsful of muira puama powder, small amounts of star anise, galangal root and cinnamon, and 3 cups of vodka. The vodka is warmed, the herbs and spices added, and the mixture bottled and left for four days, then filtered and served.

Our recipe opposite using muira puama tincture took quite a bit of processing to blend the dates and macadamia nuts, but produced a tasty cheesecake-like tart.

Ptychopetalum olacoides is a small Amazonian forest hardwood tree, with jasmine-like scented white flowers. It is the bark and root that are used

There is some confusion because another Amazonian tree, *Liriosma ovata*, is also called muira puama

The dried wood can be boiled to make a decoction, or use the powder or a tincture

Muira puama is used as a tonic for the nervous system and is antidepressant. It is considered safe, with no reported drug interactions

• stimulant

Muira puama and date tart

Process into a smooth paste:
100 ml (3½ fl oz) **muira puama tincture**,
250 g (8 oz) chopped moist **dates**, 200 g (1
cup) **macadamia nuts**.
Grease a 20 cm (8 inch) spring form tin.
Sprinkle 50 g (2 oz) **ground almonds** or
macadamia nuts evenly over the bottom of
the tin.
Spread the date mixture over it.
Whip 300 ml (10 oz) whipping **cream** until
stiff, add 1 teaspoon **vanilla extract**
and chill overnight or for at least an hour.

Nutmeg and mace are from the same tree, *Myristica fragrans*. Nutmeg is the nut, and mace is the colourful aril surrounding it

Nutmeg is also known as *rou dou kou* (China), *jaiphal* (India). Native to Moluccas or Spice Islands, Indonesia, now grown in S and SE Asia, parts of Africa and the West Indies

Also used as a sedative, and for toothache, nausea, diarrhoea and vomiting. Myristicin, the main ingredient, is toxic in large quantities; similar to MMDA in the drug Ecstasy

• relaxant

Nutmeg & mace

These two spices were once worth more than gold. Their price and exotic rarity increased their aphrodisiac reputation, but they do work

We were in south India on a tour of a spice garden. As we stopped by a nutmeg tree, our guide Krishna told us about a friend's wedding day. The groom had heard that mace was an aphrodisiac and even stronger than nutmeg, so he made sure he had lots of it. But instead of an amorous honeymoon he fell sound asleep for three days.

What the man hadn't been told is that nutmeg and mace are dose-dependent. While a little will reliably boost the libido and enhance the performance a larger amount is narcotic and conducive to sleep – Julie uses nutmeg in capsules for sleep problems.

Opening a nutmeg fruit is a sensuous experience in itself. The outer pulp is pale and fleshy, but within that comes a splash of wet, moist and lacy red fibres, the mace. This conveys nutrients to the nut, like fingers enfolding it. Sadly, like much beauty, mace fades quickly and soon dries to a dull orange.

A bag of nutmeg we bought in Zanzibar bore this somewhat enigmatic advice: 'This is better for drinks, cooking and for woman that given up strong desire for making or to fulfill their men. You have to break and inside you get nut that what we used for cooking like meat etc.' Clear?

Nutmeg nog

Heat two cups of milk or almond milk with a few squares
of white chocolate, ½ teaspoon nutmeg powder and
¼ teaspoon vanilla extract, stirring until almost boiling.
pour into cups and sprinkle a little nutmeg powder on top.

Mini mace cheesecakes

200 g (7 oz) cream cheese, warmed to room temperature
1 tablespoon icing sugar (confectioner's sugar)
½ teaspoon mace powder
¼ teaspoon vanilla extract
Mix until smooth.
Spread the mixture evenly onto 4 ginger snaps, using a
knife or your finger to smooth the edges and tops. Chill for
an hour or two before serving. (Don't leave too long or the
biscuit base may become too soft.)

Nuts & seeds

Nuts and seeds are the reproductive vehicles of plants and trees, full of the DNA and nutrition the seedling needs. Highly concentrated foods and snacks (eg salted peanuts), they make massage and eating oils (eg almond, sesame, sunflower, walnut) and other foods (eg halva and tahini from sesame, almond milk, chestnut puree)

Nutritious nuts:
eg almond, brazil, cashew, chestnut, coconut, ginkgo, hazel, hickory, macadamia, pecan, pine, pistachio, walnut

Supportive seeds:
eg linseed, mustard, pumpkin, sesame, sunflower

Some seeds have specific aphrodisiac profiles. **Pine nuts** contain testosterone, and are a male aphrodisiac in cultures from Europe and Arabia to Asia. Galen, the Greek physician to Roman emperor Marcus Aurelius, said a mixture of honey, almonds and pine nuts, eaten on three consecutive evenings, produces a surge in male vitality. Pine nuts make a good aphrodisiac garnish.

Pumpkin seeds are renowned for their high zinc content, which is needed for healthy sperm, and are a much cheaper alternative to oysters. The seeds are often used for treating prostate problems. **Sesame seeds** are known to promote breast milk in nursing mothers.

Freshly shelled nuts offer the best flavour. If you soak nuts and seeds overnight before eating this helps unlock their nutrition. Alternatively, dry-roasting them briefly in a frying pan will bring out the flavour and make grinding them easier. Use the ground form within two days for best results, and do not store for long periods.

Stuffed apricots

This recipe combines the aphrodisiac qualities of almonds with plump succulent apricots. Peaches could also be used.

Mix 50 g (1¾ oz) **ground almonds**, 2 tablespoons **maple syrup** and 1 teaspoon **orange flower water**. Divide into four, and roll each into a rough ball. Take 4 **large apricots**, slice carefully down the crease on one side and remove the pit. Place a ball of almond paste in each one and squeeze gently closed.

Bake at 180°C (350°F) for 15 minutes or until the almond paste is browning a little. Can be served with cardamom syrup (page 19).

Gomasio

Gomasio or Japanese sesame salt is a condiment made from 5 parts **black sesame seeds** (these have an earthier flavour than the white seeds) to 2 parts **sea salt**. Dry-roast the seeds, cool and grind up, together with the salt.

Oats

Oats have been cultivated for at least three thousand years. But the wildness is still there, in 'green' oats or in the creaminess of the dried version – oats are still an old smoothie

Oats have a sexy reputation. Lord Byron, for example, advised, 'When young, sow wild oats; when old, grow sage.' But what did he know? He was only 36 when he died. 'Feeling your oats' can refer to both frolicsome horses and people. Seriously, though, is there evidence that oats can make you wild?

Green oats, collected from the brief 'milky' stage of the seeds' development, are sold as an aphrodisiac. Human and animal studies show this form of oats will increase testosterone and act as a central nervous system restorative. Both green and dried oats make an excellent remedy for exhaustion, burnout and fatigue, all of which helps reduce stress and allows people's libido to revive.

Further, oats contain high levels of vitamin E, fibre and polyunsaturated fatty acids. This has two positive consequences in terms of sexual health: cholesterol levels in the blood can be lowered, and atherosclerosis (ie clogging of the blood vessels by fats) can be reduced. Freely flowing genital blood is vital for arousal in both sexes.

Oats are a nourishing food and drink – oatmilk is silky smooth and sensual – that are best enjoyed long term and regularly. Indeed porridge could be a medium for almost all the plants in this book!

Oats are also good in aphrodisiac combinations with damiana, ginseng and saw palmetto, and are restorative on the skin and in the bath.

Athol brose

This is a traditional Scottish sweet that we have adapted for this book. Normally made with whisky, it goes beautifully with herbal tinctures, in this case ginseng.

The recipe is much more delicious than it sounds! The bitterness of the ginseng disappears with the smoothing effect of the vanilla, and the cream and crunchy/chewy oats complement each other perfectly.

Toast 1 cup rolled oats in a cast iron or non-stick pan, using a medium heat until it gently browns (do not allow to burn). Meanwhile mix 2 tablespoons runny honey, 2 tablespoons ginseng tincture and 1 teaspoonful vanilla extract in a bowl.

Whip 300 ml (10 oz) double cream or whipping cream until it feels light, and stir into the bowl. Add the crunchy oatmeal just before serving, folding gently into the cream mixture. Spoon into two tall glasses.

Orange

Orange blossom has long been associated with weddings, imparting its sweetness to the occasion. Bitter orange peel stimulates the appetite

Bitter or Seville orange, *Citrus aurantium* var. *amara*; sweet orange, *Citrus aurantium* var. *dulcis*. A relative of other citrus fruits, including lemon, lime, mandarin, tangerine, satsuma, minneola, grapefuit

Parts used: bitter orange peel; bergamot oil (from bergamot oranges); leaves and twigs (as in petitgrain oil); flowers (as in neroli oil, orange flower water); whole fruit (as in Chinese medicine); and sweet orange fruit (juiced or eaten fresh)

• fragrant
• euphoric

Are oranges aphrodisiac? A morning glass of packaged orange juice isn't very sexy, but **neroli oil** certainly is. Neroli is the heady and expensive distilled oil of bitter orange flowers, emitting an uplifting, sensuous aroma that is also calming and counters depression. Use a few drops in the bath or as a massage oil with a carrier like almond oil.

Orange blossom water is the by-product of neroli distillation. It uplifts many cooked dishes, and was Victorian ladies' standby for domestic emergencies yet mild enough for babies' colic. Buy it in Middle Eastern stores or online.

Eau-de-Cologne, the famous herbal water, took orange flower water to another level.

The original eighteenth-century formula for this facial rinse combined bergamot orange oil, neroli and rosemary leaves, distilled in grape juice. Then as now good flower waters refresh your skin, and research shows they actually plump up the skin cells with nutrients, making it look and feel softer and younger.

In the **bitter orange** season (January), we made two aphrodisiac marmalades, adding yohimbe powder to one and muira puama to the other. Neither set properly (our fault for not using enough sugar), but both bore out John Evelyn's 1699 comments on bitter oranges: they 'sharpen [the] Appetite … and impart an Aromatic exceedingly grateful to the Stomach'.

Massage oils

Orange flower water is used in our stuffed figs recipe, page 35

Fragrance is an individual thing, depending on past memories and associations as much as on our actual sense of smell. Experiment to find combinations you like, but try these first if you're not sure where to start.

To a 50 ml (1¾ oz) bottle of **sweet almond oil** or **camellia oil** add 10 drops of **neroli essential oil**. Or try a combination of our favourite floral essential oils: 5 drops **neroli**, 2 drops **ylang ylang**, 2 drops **jasmine** and 3 drops **rose absolute**.

For a more earthy blend, take 50 ml (1¾ oz) of **sweet almond oil** or **camellia oil** and add 1 drop **vetiver essential oil**. To a couple of teaspoons of this base oil, add 2 drops **petit-grain essential oil** and 2 drops **sandalwood essential oil**.

65

Rose

Roses have long been a symbol of love. Their fragrance lifts the spirits and opens the heart. Roses are traditional gifts between lovers, and are associated with beauty

Roses are widely used as a flavouring in foods in the Middle East. Turkish delight, puddings and cakes are often fragranced with rosewater, and fresh rose petals can also be used in a variety of ways. Egyptian apothecaries added them in skin preparations.

Roses and chocolates given to a lover on Valentine's, or any other day, are the most powerful symbols of love our culture has found.

Roses in Christian mythology were always symbols of divine love. White roses particularly denoted purity. In the language of flowers, red roses were for passion, white for purity and yellow for friendship.

Often thought of as a feminine flower, rose benefits men as well as women, helping balance hormones and emotions. Rose treats the heart on many levels, from the physical to emotional. It is cooling, calming and astringent.

In India, rose is used to increase libido, semen production and fertility. It is also prescribed for gynaecological problems, including excessive bleeding, endometriosis, irregular periods and fibroids. It calms the nerves, and helps with depression, anxiety and headaches.

Rosa spp. The best roses for aphrodisiac purposes are strongly fragrant deep red species

Rosewater is a great skin toner, maintaining a healthy pH and moisture balance in the skin

Rose preparations are astringent, antiviral, cooling and help balance the hormones and emotions

Use the fresh flowers, rosewater, rose tincture or rose attar

- fragrant
- increases libido
- hormone balancing
- relaxing

Rose cake

Beat until creamy:
½ tablespoon **vinegar**
1 tablespoon **golden syrup**
4 tablespoons melted **butter**
½ cup light **brown sugar**
Next stir in:
½ cup **milk**
1 teaspoon **rosewater**
1 cup plain **flour**
Dissolve ½ teaspoon **bicarbonate of soda** (baking soda) in 1 tablespoon **boiling water**.
Once dissolved, stir into the cake batter. Pour into two greased and floured 20 cm (8 inch) pans.

Bake at 180°C (350°F) for 30 minutes or until done. Cool on a cake rack before turning out of the tins. Sandwich the two cakes with the rose filling and drizzle rose icing over the top.

Rose filling
Blend until creamy: a handful of chopped **rose petals**, 110 g (4 oz) soft **butter**, 100 g (3½ oz) **icing sugar**, 1 teaspoon **vanilla extract**.

Rose icing
Slowly add 2 to 3 tablespoons **rosewater** to 220 g (8 oz) **icing sugar**, beating until the consistency of thick cream.

Rose petal bath

Run a warm bath and throw in a few handfuls of **fragrant rose petals** – or for a real extravagance, use enough rose petals to completely cover the surface of the water. Light some candles and enjoy a relaxing and uplifting bath.

You can also strew your pillows or the whole bed with fresh rose petals. It worked for Cleopatra (both in real and Hollywood versions).

Rose massage

Rose attar or otto is a luxury as it takes about 30 roses to make just one drop. Use a few drops as a perfume, or mix a massage oil as below.

Add 2 drops of **rose otto** to 2 tablespoons of **camellia** or **sweet almond oil**. Use to massage your partner or yourself, or add a little in the bath. Particularly effective when rubbed over the heart.

Schisandra

Intensely flavoured schisandra berries have been used as a tonic and aphrodisiac in China for at least two thousand years

Schisandra has been revered medicinally in East Asia for thousands of years, being first described in writing in the later Han dynasty (first two centuries AD). Plants were brought to Western botanic gardens in the 1850s, and as an adaptogenic herb it has become increasingly popular in the West over the last twenty years.

Its Chinese name means 'five-flavour fruit', and you can test it for yourself with a schisandra tea made from the dried berries. Over a couple of minutes the taste intrigu-ingly develops through acrid, sour, sweet, bitter and salty – see how the sequence goes for you. We like to add liquorice to bump up the sweetness, and use the cooled tea for a wonderfully complex sangria or sorbet.

Schisandra is a famous Chinese sexual tonic, used by both sexes to help regulate bodily secretions, as in reducing night sweats, premature ejaculation and vaginal discharges. It is an effective nervous system stimulant and promoter of libido, but as an adaptogen it also works to soothe insomnia and as an antidepressant. It is taken in China for endurance and stamina in the bedroom as well as relieving stress. We recommend it as a subtle, safe, fascinating and not so inscrutable experiment.

Schisandra syrup

1 cup schisandra berries
3 cups water
Cover and simmer gently for 30 to 40 minutes. When almost cool, put in blender
and blend for a few moments.
Strain through a sieve.
Add 1 cup sugar, and bring to a boil, cooking for a couple of minutes longer.

Schisandra sorbet

Peel and slice a banana and freeze it. Also freeze 1 cup schisandra syrup (above)
mixed with the juice of 2 or 3 oranges. When frozen or nearly frozen, add the
banana to the schisandra mixture and beat with a hand blender until smooth, then
freeze again. Serve in a chilled dish.

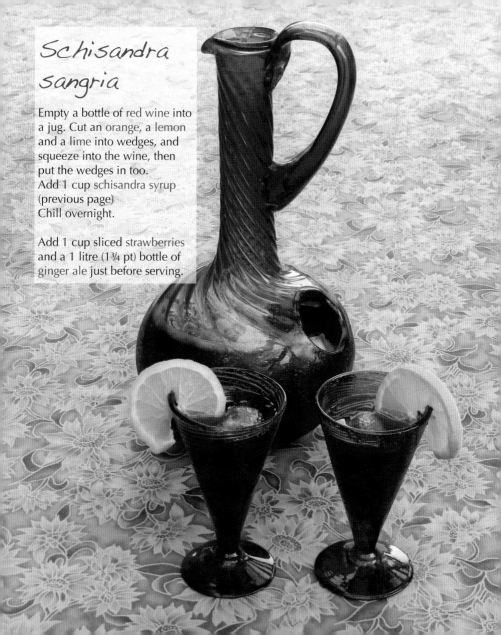

Schisandra sangria

Empty a bottle of red wine into a jug. Cut an orange, a lemon and a lime into wedges, and squeeze into the wine, then put the wedges in too.
Add 1 cup schisandra syrup (previous page)
Chill overnight.

Add 1 cup sliced strawberries and a 1 litre (1¾ pt) bottle of ginger ale just before serving.

Shatavari

Shatavari is the Ayurvedic name for wild asparagus root. Asparagus shoots are a modest aphrodisiac in Western tradition, but the Indian species has the more intriguing meaning of 'the woman with a hundred husbands'

First question: how do we decode the name? Shatavari is a female (and male) aphrodisiac, but this is best understood within a context of the care and nurturing that this herb – or many men – might give to a loved woman throughout her life.

The generalization is often made that shatavari is the leading Ayurvedic herb for the female reproductive system, as ashwagandha is for the male, although both are beneficial for each gender. Is it not remarkable that shatavari is a proven tonic for each of the female reproductive life stages of menstruation, conception, pregnancy, birth, lactation and menopause?

It achieves this breadth of action on the reproductive system by being a superb hormone and phyto-oestrogen balancer and rejuvenator. It is often called an adaptogen, a so-called 'intelligent' herb that naturally and safely harmonizes the endocrine system.

On this reading, shatavari will normalize irregular periods, increase milk flow in early pregnancy and reduce the heat of menopause. It will also heighten libido in both sexes and improve the quality of men's sperm, when the circumstances are arousing.

Shatavari is a green, thorny vine that grows throughout

Shatavari is the root of *Asparagus racemosus*, a wild asparagus native to India. It is a spiny vine that can clamber 30 feet or more up into the tree-tops

Shatavari root can be boiled in water to make a decoction, or you can use the powder or tincture

- hormone balancing
- adaptogen

73

tropical Asia. In China the roots of the equivalent asparagus, *Asparagus cochinchinensis*, known as *Tian men dong*, are used to nourish the lungs and kidneys, and as a female hormone tonic.

In Indian and Nepali tradition the roots are boiled with water or milk, clarified butter (ghee) and digestive herbs to increase shatavari's tonic properties. One standard formulation, *shatavari ghrita*, is a paste made of shatavari juice, ghee and milk, boiled together with sugar, honey and long pepper (white pepper can be substituted); ginger may be added. The paste is taken in small daily doses.

In the West, shatavari is more usually available as chopped roots or as a powder, which can be infused and drunk as a tea, or taken in tincture form. It is also an ingredient in the famous narayana massage oil, where its considerable anti-inflammatory qualities are utilized.

Shatavari electuary

An electuary is a paste made of a herb and honey. Mix **shatavari powder** with enough **runny honey** to produce a stiff paste. This can be stored in a jar and keeps for several months. Take a teaspoonful once or twice a day.

Shatavari, almond milk & saffron

Bring to boil and simmer for 7 or 8 minutes:

    2 cups **almond milk**
    2 teaspoons **shatavari powder**
    3 or 4 **cardamom pods**, crushed

Add a pinch of **saffron** and continue to simmer for half a minute longer. Strain and sweeten to taste with **brown sugar**. If you like, add a little **rosewater** before serving, and ordinary milk can be used instead of almond milk.

Woman's formula

Julie uses variations of this formula in her practice for women with low libido and low energy.

Mix tinctures of:
80 ml (3 oz) **shatavari**
40 ml (1½ oz) **rose**
30 ml (1 oz) **orange blossom**
20 ml (¾ oz) **cola nut**
20 ml (¾ oz) **cocoa**
10 ml (teaspoon) **jasmine**

Store in a dark glass bottle. Take a teaspoonful three times a day.

Tribulus
terrestris is
also known as
gokshura,
puncture vine
and land
caltrops. It is
native to Africa,
southern Europe
and Asia

Either the whole
dried plant or
just the seed
pods are used, as
a tea, tincture or
powder

It is also used for
the urinary tract,
muscle-building,
and as an
antidepressant

• hormonal
  stimulant

Tribulus

Who would have thought that this weed with nasty burs would turn out to be an important aphrodisiac? Its pretty yellow flowers carpet the ground after desert rain. Tribulus is strongly rejuvenating and strengthening

Tribulus is a yellow-flowered, summer annual weed of the Old World, with a range stretching from southern Europe, through South Asia, China and parts of Africa. It has naturalized in the Americas and Australia, often in desert areas.

Its many names are colourful, including caltrops, devil's thorn, goat head, puncture vine, *gokshura* or 'cow hoof' (India) and *bai ji li* or 'terror of the earth' (China). The reference is to the spiny fruit pods, which are so arranged that one of the sharp spikes is always upwards. The spines are strong enough to puncture tyres or pierce cows' hooves; they made a fear-some battlefield weapon both for the ancient Greeks and the Zulu warrior Shaka some two hundred years ago.

But tribulus has another reputation, especially in traditional Indian medicine, and in the modern West, as an aphrodisiac. It is nourishing and rejuvenating to the reproductive system of both genders, with its saponins and flavonoids acting as hormone precursors. It appears that the protodioscin in tribulus is readily converted to a form of testosterone (DHEA), with sexually stimulating effects.

Raising testosterone levels has the associated effect of improving muscle-building and stamina, and tribulus has been widely adopted by body-builders, especially in Bulgaria. Tribulus is also diuretic, and as a tea promotes urine where there is over-retention; it has been used for prostate problems.

In India tribulus is often combined with ashwagandha for males and with rose and shatavari for females. Our panel tried a tribulus tincture. One male (55) said: 'pleasant taste, strong arousal; lovely feeling with no irritation, and stimulation in a nice way'. A female (44) reported: 'great – it's not your usual aphrodisiac; I need to retest it'.

Tribulus is generally safe, though some users report an upset stomach. Check with a herbalist or doctor before using if you are taking antidepressants.

Tribulus balls

Grind ½ cup **sesame seed** in an electric grinder.
Add 1 teaspoon **tribulus powder**, 1 teaspoon **cardamom powder**, ¼ teaspoon **cinnamon powder**, a pinch of **black pepper** and ¼ cup **runny honey**, or enough to make a stiffish paste. Roll grape-sized bits in whole **sesame seed** to coat, then roll between your palms to make smooth balls. Chill until ready to eat. Makes about 20 balls, enough for several doses for two people.

Vanilla

The flavour of vanilla smooths and lifts recipes, both sweet and savoury, to a new level. The rich fragrance is used in many perfumes, adding an erotic depth to the blend. Experiment with it for your own aphrodisiac recipes

Vanilla is the cured seed pod of a Mexican orchid, *Vanilla planifolia*

Buy whole pods (beans), powder or real vanilla extract

• fragrant

The centuries last passed have also given the taste important exten-sion; the discovery of sugar, and its different prepara-tions, of alcoholic liquors, of wine, ices, vanilla, tea and coffee, have given us flavours hitherto unknown. – Jean Anthelme Brillat-Savarin (1755–1826)

Vanilla is such a sexy orchid that its very name is derived from the Spanish for 'little sheath' or vagina. A native of Mexico, it was an aphrodisiac for the Aztecs – Moctezuma added it to chocolate in a foamy drink that reput-edly helped him keep up with his fifty wives. Cortez and the *conquistadors* soon brought both products back to Europe, and a vanilla craze paralleled that for chocolate.

Elizabeth I, it is thought, used vanilla to flavour her favou-rite almond sweet marchpane (marzipan), and Thomas Jefferson is said to be the first American to add vanilla to ice cream. He started some-thing, as most vanilla today is produced synthetically for the US confectionery indus-try, including soft drinks; Coca-Cola, though, insists on 'the real thing' and is the main user of vanilla extract.

The perfume industry rates vanilla highly too. Perfumier Jean-Paul Guerlain says: 'My grandfather Jacques taught me to like vanilla because it adds something wonderfully erotic to a perfume. It turns Shalimar into an outrageous-ly low-cut dress.'

Yet vanilla nearly denied itself all this fame and useful-ness. When the vines were taken out of Mexico and grown elsewhere in the trop-ics, the plant usually flow-ered, but would not pollinate and give seed pods. Only by

curing fertilized pods can the active ingredient, vanillin, be released to give the unique taste and aroma we call vanilla. Another problem was that each vanilla flower lasts for only one day; if not pollinated it will die.

For three centuries the botanical world could not work out why vanilla refused to reproduce outside Mexico. Then, in 1836, a Belgian scientist discovered that a membrane in the plant kept the male and female parts separate (so this aphrodisiac plant was self-contracepting), and that a small bee was needed to effect pollination. This Melipona bee is only found in Mexico and would not relocate.

The answer came in 1841. An intuitive 12-year-old slave boy on the French island of Bourbon (now Réunion), Edmond Albius, found that he could use a pointed bamboo stick to hold the membrane aside and then with his thumb move pollen from the male to the female part. This 'geste d'Edmond' technique is still used to pollinate vanilla today, and the Indian Ocean islands are the main producers. A good worker can fertilize 2,000 vanilla flowers in a day.

Synthetic vanilla has been available since the 1870s, and the strangest things have been found to yield it, such as conifers, clovers, paper pulp

and even cow dung. **Vanilla extract** is a tincture of real vanilla pods, made with water and alcohol, and by law must contain 35% alcohol. **Vanilla essence** is distilled either from the extract, with added starch and sugar, or from an artificial source. **Vanilla powder** and **vanilla salt** are other commercial derivatives.

But the highest prices go to naturally cured **vanilla pods**, especially those with white vanillin crystals on the outside, known as 'frost' in France. The harvesting is laborious, as we noted, but so is the curing. Pollinated pods are left on the vine for up to nine months to ripen, picked by hand, immersed in hot water, and then slowly dried in the sun by day and rolled into blankets to 'sweat' by night. Final curing, when the once green and odourless bean becomes black and scented, takes months more.

The best pods are black, slightly moist, pliable and highly scented. Stored in an airtight tin, they can retain their aroma for 18 months. A good alternative is to keep one or two pods in a container of sugar, which means you will have vanilla-flavoured sugar for cakes on hand as well as the vanilla itself. The pods can be recycled several times, although one of our favourite uses is to grind part of a pod to powder with our coffee beans.

Coeur à la crème

Coeur à la crème is a traditional French recipe made in small moulds that are perforated and heart-shaped. They can be bought in kitchen shops or online. If you don't have moulds, simply drain the cheese in a lined sieve and shape by hand. Line the moulds with damp cheesecloth and let the cream cheese come to room temperature before starting. There are many different versions of this delectable dessert.

Beat together: 200 g (9 oz) package **cream cheese** (pour off any liquid first), ½ cup **crème fraîche** or **ricotta cheese**, 4 tablespoons **icing sugar**, ½ teaspoon grated **lemon zest**, and the seeds scraped from the inside of a **vanilla bean**.
Press into the lined moulds, and chill overnight. To serve, turn the hearts out onto a plate and drizzle with **passionfruit**, as below, or add your favourite strawberry or raspberry sauce, or fresh berries in season.

Ylang ylang

Ylang ylang in Malay means 'flower of flowers'. The yellow-green blossoms have a rich, sensuous fragrance, and their oil is used in many aphrodisiac blends and high-quality perfumes. The effect is euphoric and languorous. It is a scent that makes you smile

Ylang ylang blossoms themselves look so relaxed that they seem about to droop off the branch. Their seductive scent evokes tropical heat and lethargy, removing tension while stimulating the senses.

If you are in the tropics, you can use fresh ylang ylang flowers to scent a room, clothes or your hair. The flowers were traditionally strewn on the beds of newly weds in Indonesia.

In colder climes the essential oil is the usual way to buy ylang ylang. A few drops can be added to coconut oil for a sensuous body massage; this mix was prized in Victorian times as macassar oil, used as a male hair conditioner.

The best form to buy is steam-distilled and is known as ylang ylang 'extra'. This is taken from the first distillation, and is more costly, but well worth insisting on. What price euphoria?

Bath truffles

Cocoa butter is a wonderful neutral carrier for aromatic oils and fragrances, with an uncanny quality of melting at precisely the same temperature as our blood heat. This means the 'truffles' will be solid at room temperature but melt readily in the bath.

One aromatic bath truffle dissolved in your bath will make your skin feel soft and velvety, while the ylang ylang is absorbed effortlessly as you relax in the heat.

Melt 75 g (3 oz) **cocoa butter**
Add 20 to 30 drops of **ylang ylang essential oil**
Pour into heart-shaped chocolate moulds, or an ice cube tray.
Chill in the fridge until firmly set, then turn out. Store in a jar in a cool place.

To use, drop a truffle in a warm bath and allow it to melt. Be careful stepping in, as everything will become sensually slippery and slithery.

Yohimbe

Yohimbe is among the top five aphrodisiacs for name recognition, along with (arguably) horny goat weed, ginseng, Spanish fly and oysters. It is powerful, dangerously so in overdose, and we recommend using it with caution and respect

Yohimbe is the local name for the bark of a large tree from tropical West Africa. Taken as yohimbe powder, and in its extract form yohimbine hydrochloride, this is one of the best-known aphrodisiacs.

Until US law was changed in the 1980s yohimbine, the extracted chemical, was the only Food and Drug Administration-approved over-the-counter 'natural' aphrodisiac. Yohimbine is now a prescription-only drug for male sexual dysfunction in the US, and in the UK is available from registered pharmacists and approved professionals. Yohimbe the plant can be bought from herbalists, or as capsules in pharmacies and health stores. If you purchase online, you need to be sure that you are getting authentic, unadulterated yohimbe.

Yohimbe is still used in its source areas in celebration and ritual, with yohimbe tea being drunk before ceremonies with drums, fires and dancing begin, followed by vigorous coupling. Yohimbe is a central nervous system stimulant and in larger quantities is mildly hallucinogenic, so if it's wild dancing and ecstatic sexual experience you seek, it could be the aphrodisiac for you.

You should be aware that yohimbe is dose-dependent: too low a dose for your personal physiology and psychology and little happens; too much in your specific circumstances can cause unpleasant side effects such as raised blood pressure, heart palpitations, nausea, insomnia and uneasiness. Both yohimbe and yohimbine should be avoided if you have a history of coronary heart disease, stroke, high blood pressure, migraine and panic attacks, or if you are pregnant or nursing. If in any doubt, ask your doctor or a herbalist before you take yohimbe/yohimbine.

At the right dosage, the extract yohimbine (little research has been done on yohimbe as such) has been found in human and animal studies to increase frequency of sexual activity and to heighten sexual arousal; yohimbine also counteracts the turn-off feeling left by many antidepressants. Expect skin tingling and shivers down your spine, expanded awareness and the feeling of blood flow to your genital area within a few minutes of taking the right dosage, and the effects will last up to about four hours.

Yohimbe has its risks, as we hope we have made clear. At the same time, and unusually among familiar aphrodisiacs, it has a clinical track record for treating male sexual dysfunction and a long tradition of ritual sexualized use in its African setting.

Yohimbe bought for teas resembles a dried leaf mulch – red-brown, dusty and somewhat oily. Start with a teaspoon for a large cup of boiling water and brew for 5 minutes. Some people like to add a teaspoon of vitamin C to moderate the rather acrid taste. You can also buy yohimbe in capsule and extract form, but you do know less about the quality, strength and reliability of these processed products than when you can obtain the dried herb from a reputable supplier.

Yo cake

Warm until soft: ½ tablespoon **vinegar**
                                  1 tablespoon **golden syrup**
                                  4 tablespoons **butter**
                                  ½ cup **light brown sugar**

Beat until creamy, then stir in: ½ cup **milk**
                                    2 teaspoons **ground ginger**
                                    1 teaspoon **yohimbe powder**
                                    1 cup **flour**

Dissolve ½ teaspoon **bicarbonate of soda** (baking soda)
in 1 tablespoon **boiling water**
Once dissolved, stir into the cake batter.

Pour into 2 greased and floured 20 cm (8 inch) pans.
Bake at 180 degrees for half an hour.

Part 2
Other Aphrodisiacs

In a short book we have had to be severely selective, but we did want to mention other significant aphrodisiacs in this second part. Kava kava is here but would have been in the main section if it hadn't been proscribed in England a few years back, depriving us temporarily of one of the best euphorics; black pepper, ginkgo and saw palmetto were next in line for our main list had there been room.

We are including many other plants because they occur in aphrodisiac formulas sold on the Internet, the way most people buy their aphrodisiacs. We feel it important to offer some explanation of what these plants are, even in this very brief form, so that buyers have more knowledge to inform their purchase.

To compile our list we surveyed 100 current (February 2011) websites that fulfilled two conditions: first a listing in the top 100 or so hits for the search terms 'herbal aphrodisiac' or 'herbal Viagra', and secondly botanical constituents itemized. Both 'male' and 'female' interest sites were checked, and there was no control for place of origin, number of items in an aphrodisiac mixture or type of herb: the criterion was popularity. Bear in mind that this was an informal survey and that things change rapidly in the virtual world. It is a snapshot of the most popular plant aphrodisiacs on the currently most popular buying medium.

We found horny goat weed to be the runaway leader with 52 citations in 100 formulas, followed by panax ginseng with 34, damiana and ginkgo 31 each, tribulus 28, muira puama 27, the amino acid L-arginine 26, maca 25, tongkat ali and yohibme 21, and saw palmetto 20. Also in our top twenty most popular online aphrodisiacs were ashwagandha, catuaba, oats, rhodiola, schisandra, shatavari, Siberian ginseng, velvet bean and wild yam. We have covered all these along with others that scored at least two hits in our survey.

Listing is by common name in English where possible, but where the name used in commerce is in another language, that is preferred.

Agnus castus *Vitex agnus castus*
Chaste tree, Monk's pepper leaves,
berries make herbal tea or tincture;
once thought to be aphrodisiac for
women and anaphrodisiac for men,
but effects vary with dosage
Areca nut *Areca catechu* seed of
the tropical areca palm, also called
betel nut; usually rolled into betel
leaf, making a mildly aphrodisiac
stimulant favoured in S and SE Asia
Artichoke *Cynara cardunculus* a
thistle from the Mediterranean, the
boiled flower buds and heart of the
globe artichoke are aphrodisiac in
reputation and what fun to eat!
Asparagus *Asparagus officinalis* the
shoots eaten as a vegetable have a
persistent aphrodisiac reputation.
Culpeper (1653) wrote that the shoots
'stirreth up bodily lust in man or
woman'
Astragalus *Astragalus membranaceus/
propinquus* Milk vetch, Huang qi root
is an energizing tonic
Ayahuasca *Banisteriopsis caapi* Caapi
Yage Amazonian vine used in ritual
psychotropic beverages; vomiting
often precedes 'high'

Ba ji tian *Morinda officinalis* Morinda
a Chinese root used for impotence,
infertility and related problems
Bala *Sida cordifolia* Country mallow
native to India, has high ephedrine
content, making it stimulatory to the
heart and genital blood flow

Black cohosh *Cimifuga racemosa
Actaea racemosa* Black snakeroot root
in native American herbal lore treated
multiple ailments; now used for PMT
and menopause treatments, and as a
female aphrodisiac
Brahmi *Bacopa monnieri* Water hyssop
marshland succulent used in China
and India as a sexual tonic
Butea *Butea superba* Red kwao krua
vine native to Thailand, whose roots
make a popular mild aphrodisiac
locally and in last twenty years sold
online; called a 'miracle drug'

Calamus *Acorus calamus* Sweet flag
roots of this wetland plant have been
a popular tonic and aphrodisiac in
China, India and Egypt for millennia;
banned from 1968 in US for use in
food, but this is one strain only, and
three are widely used medicinally
Catuaba *Erythroxylum vaccinifolium*
or *Trichilia catigua* two rainforest
plants with aphrodisiac reputations,
both known as catuaba: in the state
of Minas people say 'Until a father
reaches 60, the child is his; after that,
the child is catuaba's.' A love tonic
Cistanche *Cistanche deserticola* Rou
cong rong the fleshy stem of Chinese
broomrape is aphrodisiac and a sexual
tonic for both sexes
Clavo huasca *Tynanthus panurensis*
Clove vine root and bark of a South
American vine, aphrodisiac and
stimulant; a key ingredient in local
aphrodisiac *rompe calzon*, 'bust your

britches'. Popular drink in USA
Coco de mer *Lodoicea maldivica* endangered palm from the Maldives, with a suggestively shaped nut; not used as an aphrodisiac
Common curciligo *Curculigo orchioides* Golden eye-grass Xian mao rhizome of this Chinese plant is a sexual tonic
Cordyceps *Cordyceps sinensis* Caterpillar fungus, Dong chong xia cao (translated as 'winter insect, summer grass'): fruiting body of a Tibetan fungus that is parasitic on caterpillars; used as a sexual tonic

Dodder *Cuscuta epithymum* Cuscuta, Tu si zi the seed of this Chinese parasitic plant is a sexual tonic
Dong quai *Angelica sinensis* Female ginseng the root regulates menstruation and is a blood tonic

Eleuthero *Eleutherococcus senticosus* Siberian ginseng this root was the first plant to be called an adaptogen, after much Soviet research; a sexual tonic

Ferula *Ferula hermonis* Zallouh, Lebanese viagra resin and tincture of root long used as tonic and aphrodisiac in Mediterranean; found to stimulate oestrogen *and* testosterone; also mood elevating

Galangal *Alpinia galanga* Blue ginger, Kaempferia ginger-like rhizome,

called *kah* in Thai cuisine, has similar warming and tonic effects to ginger
Gardenia *Gardenia jasminoides, G. augusta, G. taitensis* zhi zi the heavenly smell of the white flowers is perfect for weddings; in Tahiti mixed with coconut oil to make sensuous *monoi de Tahiti*, a superior bath truffle
Garlic chives *Allium tuberosum* Chinese leek a warming seed used for sexual weakness
Ginkgo *Ginkgo biloba* Yin xing leaves of this ancient tree improve circulation, including in the brain (used for Alzheimer's); taken as tincture it helps in erectile problems
Gotu kola *Centella asiatica/Hydrocotyle asiatica* Brahmi, Chi hsueh ts'ao an adaptogen and circulatory stimulant; also for memory, tissue regeneration
Guaraná *Paullinia cupana* South American vine with high caffeine content, more a heart tonic than aphrodisiac; for endurance; Brazilian national drink is guarana soda

He shou wu *Polygonum multiflorum* Fo ti, Chinese knotweed root is a rejuvenating tonic
Honey (bee pollen & royal jelly) the oldest natural sweetener, long associated with sex (think honeymoon); bee pollen is an energy superfood and libido enhancer, royal jelly a fertility-supporting antiviral; mead and hydromel are alcoholic forms; so-called 'nectar of Aphrodite'

Iboga *Tabernanthe iboga* roots of a rainforest shrub from Central Africa; small doses stimulate nervous system, larger doses are hallucinogenic

Jequirity *Abrus precatorius* Crab's eye, Ratti, Xiang si dou ('mutual love bean') red seed of a vetch-like tropical vine: beautiful but poisonous – avoid!

Jujube *Ziziphus ziziphus* Red date, Chinese date [or *Z. mauritiana* Indian jujube] fruit of small spiny tree; a calming, nourishing tonic

Kava kava *Piper methysticum* vine related to pepper; root important in Pacific island cultures as a relaxing and euphoric beverage

Lycium *Lycium chinensis* Wolfberry, Matrimony vine is not a vine at all, but a rambling bush; berries are marketed as a tonic and superfood

Nettle *Urtica dioica* seed is tonic and may be aphrodisiac, root helps prostate problems, leaves are highly nutritious; a wonder wild weed

Palmarosa *Cymbopogon martinii* Indian geranium, Rosha grass related to lemongrass and citronella, yields an aphrodisiac essential oil

Passionfruit *Passiflora edulis* Granadilla fruit of this tropical vine is delicious and full of seeds; good juice for aphrodisiac recipes

Patchouli *Pogostemon cablin* leaves of tropical plant give the essential oil, famous in the 1960s, used in many perfumes; a grounding aphrodisiac

Pepper *Piper nigrum* Black pepper fruit of this tropical Indian vine is the familiar spice; stimulates appetite and circulation. Isabel Allende writes: 'I go on record as saying that it brings joy to widows and alleviates the impotence of the timid'

Pomegranate *Punica granatum* a small Mediterranean tree; red seeds and juice a famed tonic and aphrodisiac

Prickly ash *Xanthoxylum fraxineum* (*Zanthoxylum americanum*) the bark tincture improves blood circulation

Pumpkin *Cucurbita maxima* Winter squash seeds a good source of zinc and essential fatty acids, beneficial for prostate and sperm health; easy to find in shops and cheap too

Pygeum *Pygeum africanum* bark of this African tree is used for treating prostate problems

Quebracho *Aspidosperma quebracho-blanco* bark of tree from northern Argentina, contains yohimbine; aphrodisiac and mild antidepressant; banned in some countries

Rhodiola *Rhodiola rosea* Golden root, Rose root root of a plant from

Northern Europe and Asia; an adaptogen, which heightens memory, mood and sexual performance

Saffron *Crocus sativus* **the stigmas of this autumn-flowering crocus from Morocco, Greece and Spain make the world's most expensive spice; antidepressant and mood uplifting**
Sandalwood *Santalum album* a semi-parasitic tree that after growing 30 years gives divinely smelling essential oils; a calming aphrodisiac
Sarsaparilla *Smilax officinalis* old US traditions of using this vine root for sexual dysfunction were confirmed by 1939 discovery that it contains testosterone; use for limited periods
Sassafras *Sassafras albidum* a tonic and aphrodisiac tea is made from the roots; avoid the extracted safrole oil in large dosage
Saw palmetto *Serenoa repens* berry of Carribbean palm; sexual tonic, often used for prostate problems; safe and adaptable, mixed with other tonics
Skirret *Sium sisarum* Crummock root vegetable in carrot family, considered 'provoking unto venery' in old herbals; tasty and easy to grow
Suoyang *Cynomorium songaricum, C. coccineum,* Yang locker, Tarthuth the fleshy stem of this Chinese, European and Arabian parasitic plant is aphrodisiac and a sexual tonic

Tongkat ali *Eurycoma longifolia* Pasak bumi, Eurycoma small tree from

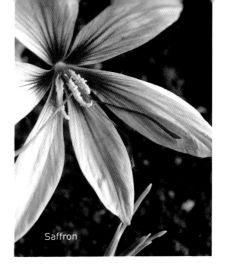
Saffron

SE Asia; increases sexual desire, enhances performance and general well-being, but products on market often adulterated; endangered
Truffles (the fungus) have intense flavour and aroma, are incredibly costly and strongly aphrodisiac. In France called 'the testicle of the earth'. 'If a man is rich enough to eat many, slightly cooked under the embers, his loves will be many.' Truffles in infused olive oil are more affordable

Velvet bean *Mucuna pruriens* Cowage, Nescafé, Kapikacchu legume, an aphrodisiac of ancient India, used for erectile problems; contains L-dopa, and now treats Parkinson's

Vetiver *Chrysopogon zizanioides* Khus perennial grass native to India; roots yield an earthy, sensual essential oil

Wild yam *Dioscorea villosa* American vine from whose root testosterone and progesterone are manufactured; the body cannot do this unaided, so beware claims of 'natural' wild yam as a beneficial steroidal hormone

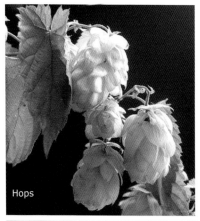

Hops

Anaphrodisiacs
In case some of the recipes we give are just too stimulating, you may need an anaphrodisiac, or libido buster. 'Cold' plants like cucumber, lettuce and wild lettuce have long been used in this way in Western herbal medicine, along with agnus castus, hops, dill seed and rue. But do bear in mind Ovid's lament from two thousand years ago:
Alas! There are no herbs to cure love

Helpful supplements

DHEA
(5-dehydroepiandrosterone)
an important sex hormone and precursor of testosterone; DHEAS is the sulfate (stored) form; taken as a supplement to raise testosterone

L-arginine, L-histidine, L-tyrosine
three of the amino acids involved in the human sexual response, taken as supplements; L-arginine is converted to nitric oxide, increasing blood flow to the genitals; L-histidine activates histamine, involved in genital blood surges and orgasm; L-tyrosine stimulates L-dopa in the brain to boost sexual desire

Vitamin B complex among the B vitamins involved in sexual response are B_5 in stamina; B_{12} in sperm production; niacin in blood flow to the genitals; choline, a neurotransmitter in sexual arousal

Vitamin C research suggests low levels of vitamin C (ascorbic acid) lead to DNA damage in sperm, while supplementation or increased C through fresh fruit and vegetables improves sperm health and motility

Zinc an important element for production of testosterone and for preventing prostate problems; pine nuts, almonds and pumpkin seeds are good sources, or use supplements

Resources

Recommended UK suppliers
Artemis Herbs (Western herbs, tinctures, oils, aromatic waters) www.artemisherbs.co.uk 01570 471000
The Natural Dispensary (complementary supplements, remedies) naturaldispensary.co.uk 01453 757792
Pukka Herbs (organic herbs, Ayurvedic supplier) www.pukkaherbs.com 0845 3751744
Tree-harvest (one-stop source for the herbs in this book, oils, nuts, seeds, etc) www.tree-harvest.com 01531 650764

Finding a professional herbalist
Association of Master Herbalists www.associationofmasterherbalists.co.uk
College of Practitioners of Phytotherapy www.phytotherapists.org
The International Register of Consultant Herbalists and Homoeopaths www.irch.org
National Institute of Medical Herbalists www.nimh.org.uk
Unified Register of Herbal Practitioners www.urhp.co.uk

Further reading
Allende, Isabel, *Aphrodite: A memoir of the senses* (London: Flamingo, 1999)

Buhner, Stephen Harrod, *The Natural Testosterone Plan: For sexual health and energy* (Rochester, VT: Healing Arts Press, 2007)

Connell, Charles, *Aphrodisiacs in Your Garden* (London: Arthur Barker, 1965)

De Luca, Diana, *Botanica Erotica: Arousing body, mind and spirit* (Rochester, VT: Healing Arts Press, 1998)

Hopkins, Martha & Lockridge, Randall, *InterCourses: An aphrodisiac cookbook* (Waco, TX: Terrace Publishing, 1997; 2nd edn, 2007)

Kilham, Chris, *Hot Plants: Nature's proven sex boosters for men and women* (New York: St Martin's Griffin, 2004)

Melville, Francis, *Love Potions & Charms: Over 50 ways to seduce, bewitch, and cherish your lover* (London: Simon & Schuster, 2001)

Rätsch, Christian, *Plants of Love: The history of aphrodisiacs and a guide to their identification and use* (Berkeley, CA: Ten Speed Press, 1997)

Taylor, Leslie, *The Healing Power of Rainforest Herbs: A guide to understanding and using herbal medicinals* (Garden City, NY: Square One Publishers, 2005)

Tisserand, Maggie, *Essential Oils for Lovers: A sensual guide to aromatherapy* (London: HarperCollins, 1999)

Winston, David & Maimes, Steven, *Adaptogens: Herbs for strength, stamina, and stress relief* (Rochester, VT: Healing Arts Press, 2007)

Index

Credits

This project has been ten years in the making, going through such possible formats as a cookbook or a reference text on the world's herbal aphrodisiacs. We are grateful to many people and gardens along the way, notably in Australia, Cyprus, India, Namibia, the USA and Zanzibar. We owe particular thanks to our publishers, Merlin Unwin and Karen McCall, for believing in us and focusing us on a shorter but finally realizable practical guide to making your own aphrodisiacs.

Special thanks go to Janice and Ed Swab and Joe Hollis in North Carolina, Said Mohammed in Zanzibar and Thomas Tomichen in Kerala for their kindness in helping us identify and photograph many of the plants featured in this book, and also to Jennifer Holland who got our damiana plant to flower in her greenhouse. All photographs are by Julie Bruton-Seal and in her copyright.

Thanks to Christine Herbert and Karin Haile for checking the manuscript, and to a panel of friends who tested some of the recipes.

photo by Mary Plage

The authors
Julie Bruton-Seal is a practising medical herbalist and naturopath, photographer, author and artist. She collaborated with her husband Matthew ('my favourite author!') on *Hedgerow Medicine* (published in the USA as *Backyard Medicine*) (2008) and *Kitchen Medicine* (2010). They live in Norfolk, UK,

Matthew Seal is an editor, writer and proofreader, and has worked on books, magazines and newspapers in England and South Africa – 'none has been as much fun as working with Julie'.

Our website: www.hedgerowmedicine.com